Rotterdam
Architecture
City

Paul Groenendijk, Piet Vollaard
photography: Ossip van Duivenbode

nai010 publishers

Welcome to Rotterdam

This guide, featuring the 100 most noteworthy buildings, from the Laurenskerk to the Markthal, provides a representative overview of Rotterdam architecture. But this city is more than just its buildings. So the selection has been augmented with the finest gardens and parks and with a list of art in public space. Anecdotes, quotations and historical details at the bottom of the pages, generally related to the building concerned or its immediate surroundings, enrich the visitor's experience of the city. A number of thematic chapters consider urban development, the cultural scene and nightlife.
Want to see more? Visit www.architectureguide.nl, a database created by the makers of this guide containing over 2000 Dutch buildings, including around 450 in Rotterdam. Or visit (and like) us on Facebook: facebook.com/architectuurgids. For a special Rotterdam tour including guides and/or cycle hire, see www.urbanguides.nl.

Contents

Stationsplein 1
Team CS (Benthem Crouwel,
Meyer & Van Schooten, West 8)
1999-2013

Increased passenger numbers, the arrival of the high-speed train and the extension of the metro line necessitated the replacement of Sybold van Ravesteyn's much-loved 1957 station. At the same time, the entire station precinct was reconfigured and a car park was built beneath Kruisplein. In a configuration also common in the nineteenth century, the new station comprises two dovetailing sections: concourse and platform covering.

The latter consists of a glazed roof resting on timber joists and supported by Y-shaped columns. On the north side this glass roof folds into a taut glass facade. The triangular station hall has an angled and dramatically cantilevered roof whose pointed end almost touches Weena. The sloping line of the facade ensures that the Groothandelsgebouw 2, a post-war reconstruction icon, remains visible. The concourse ceiling is clad with timber siding, the exterior of the roof with crumpled stainless steel sheeting.

Speculaasjes

A few references to the old CS have been incorporated into the new station. The artworks that flanked the wings of the old station, dubbed 'speculaasjes' because of their resemblance to Dutch spice cookies, reappear on platforms 1 and 15 above the entrance to the bicycle tunnel. Echoes of this distinctive shape are to be found in the pattern of the concrete elements in the concourse wall and even in the solar cells on the glass roof. As it happens, the original 'artworks' were realized without any artistic involvement. It is said that Van Ravesteyn had wanted to engage the sculptor Henry Moore, but owing to cost-cutting measures the provisional shapes on the construction drawings were simply copied.

2 Groothandelsgebouw

Stationsplein 45
H.A. Maaskant, W. van Tijen
1945-1952
J. & A.J. van Stigt (rest. 2000-2005)

This multi-company megastructure of 128,000 m² was the start and remains the symbol of Rotterdam's post-war reconstruction. At the time of delivery the vast block (220 x 84 x 43 m.) was the largest building in the Netherlands. But its air of monumentality is only partly ascribable to its size; a more important factor is the rational, repetitive application of just concrete and glass to facades of an almost classical architectural detailing and modelling. The building's mass is broken up by three courtyards and shot through with internal service streets. Its main entrance faces onto the station forecourt with four secondary entrances set on both sides of the two building parts separating the three courtyards. Retail spaces occupy the ground floor of the building's outer sides. The remaining spaces are fitted out as storerooms and freely subdivisible office and sales areas. Passenger and goods lifts and galleries around the courtyards deal with the internal circulation. Collective amenities including the famous Engels café-restaurant cluster round the main entrance. Much thought has been given to modelling the facades so that the building with its repetition of cladding units does not appear unduly monolithic. Two shared rooftop canteens and a common terrace stand atop the building. Ten years after delivery, the concrete frame of the rooftop pavilion above the main entrance was completed as a cinema. Here, the large window on the city behind the stage and film screen is still one of Rotterdam's major surprises. The Groothandelsgebouw was restored to its original state by the Van Stigt firm of restoration architects.

Maaskant and a fellow Rotterdammer are standing among the ruins the day after the bombardment. 'Sir, we are looking at our city's grave,' the man sobs. 'No,' replies Maaskant, 'we are looking at its glory.'

B. van Dommelen, Portret van H.A. Maaskant, 1983

Delftseplein 31
E.H.A. & H.M.J.H. Kraaijvanger
1954-1959
Claus & Kaan (ren. 2005-2010)

The Rotterdam architects Evert and Herman Kraaijvanger played an active part in post-war reconstruction work. Having started out using a traditional idiom, in this station post office they switched to a more rational style based on the functional layout of the building. Automation for this railway post office meant tall work areas with a minimum of columns. Its width of 34 metres is spanned in concrete supported by just one central column. There are less-tall office storeys on the east and west sides. In the double-height work areas, the scale is determined by a horizontal window rising 2.1 metres. The uppermost level, 9.5 metres high and without columns, is clearly expressed in the facade by brick and concrete architecture typical of the post-war reconstruction. The sorting office's relocation to the city outskirts rendered the building redundant. As Central Post, the renovated building provides office space for the creative industry, to which end mezzanine floors were inserted in the double-height storeys. Public-oriented uses such as cafés, restaurants and a health club occupy the ground floor.

'Give us walls'

The local 'Groep r' artists who made this demand immediately after the war got their wish: a lot of Rotterdam post-war reconstruction architecture features wall art. The most spectacular example is the mosaic by Louis van Roode stretching the full height of Central Post. From the 1970s onwards, many blank walls in the old Rotterdam neighbourhoods were painted by artists and although many have since disappeared as a result of demolition, just as many have appeared on new blank walls.

Weena 505
A. Bonnema
1986-1991

For years the Weena had been an empty expanse in the city centre. Then within the space of five years it burgeoned into a metropolitan boulevard complete with high-rise along American lines. The street profile has been narrowed by the development on the north side above the metro tube, and by a new front line of buildings on the south side. Most of the buildings are offices, with only part of the planned housing seeing the light of day. The south side of Weena has had several buildings designed along it in front of the existing street elevation, narrowing the boulevard from 90 metres to 60. Thrusting up 151 metres, the headquarters of the Nationale-Nederlanden insurance group, Delftse Poort, was from 1991 till 2010 the country's tallest office building. The brief was to design two potentially independent office towers of 36,000 and 24,000 square metres on a shared base containing the entrance, a company restaurant, a training and conference centre and a sports hall; the brief also called for a parking facility for 1200 cars. The two office slabs of 151 and 93 metres stand on columns either side of the metro running beneath the site on a table-like structure. They have a clear span of 14.4 metres. The facades consist of structural members in precast concrete with a finish of solar reflective glazing. Cores, each containing a lift and stairs, and external buttresses provide stability. These are clad in black neoparies, a product of crystallized glass as hard as granite. Since 2015 the building has been used mainly as a business complex with the company restaurant becoming a public food court.

Architecture on Weena

J. Hoogstad, Unilever Headquarters, Weena 455, 1988-1992
J. Hoogstad, Housing Block, Weena 381-443, 1987-1990
H. Klunder, Office/Housing Block, Weena 181-323, 1982-1990
H. Klunder, Weenahuis, Weena 119-173, 1983-1987
C.G. Dam, Housing Block, Weena 89-115, 1981-1984
ZZ&P, Stad Rotterdam Headquarters, Weena 70, 1985-1990
H.A. Maaskant, F.W. de Vlaming, Hilton Hotel, Weena 10, 1960-1964
J.J.M. Klompenhouwer (Brouwer Steketee), Office Building, Weena 200, 1986-1993
H.A. Maaskant, Weena Building, Weena-Zuid 106-178, 1966-1968
Ellerman, Lucas, Van Vugt, Plaza Complex, Weena 660, 1984-1992
Webb, Zerafa, Menkes, Housden, Millennium Tower, Weena 686, 1997-2000

History of the city

Until the middle of the nineteenth century, Rotterdam was a modest town in the shadow of Dordrecht, Schiedam and Delft. The dam in the River Rotte from which the settlement took its name was probably built around 1270. Rotterdam was granted city rights on 7 June 1340, at which time it was home to some 1000 people. In the middle of the sixteenth century the city experienced a surge in growth. Trade and industry developed and between 1550 and 1600 the population doubled to 13,000. It was during this period that the *Stadsdriehoek* (urban triangle) took shape and the first docks were built. With the passing of the Golden Age the city's spatial development stagnated in the seventeenth and eighteenth centuries.

The railway links with Amsterdam, Utrecht and Antwerp and the opening of Nieuwe Waterweg shipping canal in 1872 were crucial to Rotterdam's development into a major port city. Docks and wharves were enlarged and surrounding municipalities annexed. Thousands of immigrants from the rural hinterland were drawn to the city by the prospect of work. From the second half of the nineteenth century the population increased dramatically to 300,000 in 1900 and 450,000 in 1915. The population explosion precipitated a boom in jerry-built housing with builders displaying great ingenuity in circumventing the National Housing Act of 1901. Both the Municipal Housing Agency and private parties endeavoured to build good quality housing: Justus van Effen Complex **51**, Kiefhoek **91**, Heijplaat **98** and Vreewijk garden village **92**. Between the two world wars, Rotterdam became the cradle of Nieuwe Bouwen (Dutch Modernism), with architects like J.J.P. Oud, Brinkman & Van der Vlugt, Willem van Tijen and Jo van den Broek, and important projects like the Van Nelle Factory **52**, Feijenoord Stadium **94** and the Bergpolderflat **56**.

At the beginning of the Second World War, Rotterdam was devastated by a German bombing raid. As soon as the rubble had been cleared away the city architect, W.G. Witteveen was charged with producing a reconstruction plan, although in the end it was his assistant, Cornelis van Traa, who finished the Basic Plan for Reconstruction. He abandoned the idea of reconstructing the historical city centre and instead designed a completely new spatial layout with a radical separation of functions that took account of the growing importance of traffic. The appearance and character of the city centre was largely determined by the reconstruction project. Houses were built mainly on the outskirts of the city in a series of new residential areas that displayed a trend towards a larger scale in terms of housing (high-rise), green space and roads. That larger scale was also evident in the first urban renewal projects in Crooswijk, Oude Noorden and Cool at the end of the 1960s. Before long,

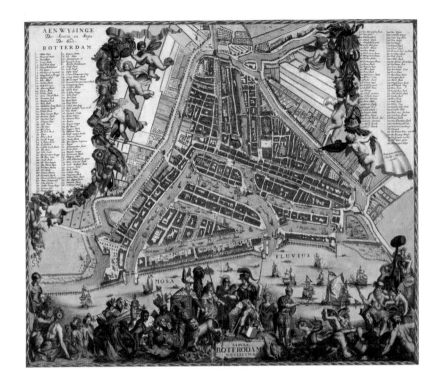

however, under the influence of local protests, urban renewal began to be characterized by respect for the existing structure and for the wishes of the residents, resulting in renovation and small-scale new construction. Attempts were also made to improve the liveliness and ambience of the city centre by building cheery, small-scale dwellings, constructing terraces and pavilions, introducing more greenery and freezing office construction.

Development stagnated due to the oil crisis in 1973, but took off again in the middle of the 1980s when the construction of the World Trade Center on top of the Stock Exchange **18** led to the growing realization that high-rise and commercial activities contributed significantly to the dynamism of a city. The city centre was speedily completed and obsolete docklands and industrial areas were transformed into modern residential districts. As a result of the vigorous development of Kop van Zuid **72**, the centre of the city shifted to the banks of the river, with the new Erasmus Bridge **70** providing a contemporary logo. The banks of the River Maas also proved an attractive location for housing, while the centre received fresh impetus from the exponents of fun shopping, the Koopgoot **14** and the Markthal **25**. A lot of post-war reconstruction architecture enjoyed a second lease of life courtesy of adaptive reuse.

5 Schieblock ☕ 🍴

Schiekade 189
ZUS (Zones Urbaines Sensibles)
2009
Brouwer & Deurvorst (orig. des. 1959);
ZUS (Luchtsingel 2011-2014)

Plans for the large-scale redevelopment of the area between the railway line and the high-rise along Weena 🔲 as far as the Rotterdam Central District business centre came to nothing after the 2008 financial crisis. To stem rising vacancy rates and the decline of the area, ZUS developed a strategy for temporary occupancy of the empty Schieblock office, and for a new 'air bridge' connection with the former Hofplein station 🔲 on the other side of the railway line. An array of creative enterprises set up shop in the Schieblock and partly due to the success of that venture, the temporary use was extended by five years in 2014. Thanks to Stadsinitiatief, a municipal grant scheme decided by public ballot, a wooden bridge was built right through the Schieblock to Hofbogen, including a park on the Pompenburg wasteland, and a link was made with the redevelopment of the Hofplein viaduct, abandoned since 2012.

Dakakker

Since the economic crisis, Rotterdammers have enthusiastically embraced various forms of temporary green space and urban farming on a variety of empty plots in the city. For its part, the city council pursues a policy of greening the many flat roofs in the city. Both developments coalesce in Dakakker 🔲, a vegetable and herb garden on the roof of the Schieblock, which also hosts an apiary. Local residents are informed about the practicalities of green roofs and urban farming and motivated to get involved through harvest festivals, tastings and courses.

6   Bouwcentrum

Kruisplein 15
J.W.C. Boks
1946-1948
Schiller Architects (ren. 2000)

The original 16-sided exhibition build-ing of the Bouwcentrum (Building Centre) is largely hidden from view by offices and exhibition areas added later. From the core, a mushroom floor on eight columns, three concrete bridges extend radially to the per-imeter, which on the ground floor con-tains offices and on the upper floor enclosed exhibition areas off a pro-jecting gallery. The core has a con-crete dome roof inlaid with glass bricks. The exhibition section has been restored and is now used as office space. The buildings that housed the now relocated Bouwcentrum have been partly renovated and partly demolished. Henry Moore's brick sculpture has been relocated to the new First Rotterdam extension by architect Frits van Dongen.

Brick art

British sculptor Henry Moore designed a brick relief artwork for the Bouwcentrum facade. Wall Relief No. 1 **A2**, a complex work consisting of 16,000 handmade vari-coloured bricks, was executed by master bricklayers in 1954. Under threat by the planned demolition of the old high-rise, the artwork will now have a place in the new building.

West-Kruiskade, Nieuwe
Binnenweg & environs
Aktiegroep Het Oude Westen
with P.P. Hammel
1970-1993

A 19th-century district, Oude Westen was once characterized by long, narrow streets of jerry-building. In the early 1970s its slow decline was called to a halt when inhabitants together with a number of architects set up an action committee and demanded that the district be renovated and restructured in the interest of its residents. No swathe of demolition then, but renovations, restorations and small-scale redevelopment with rents locals could afford. This process has since been institutionalized as 'urban renewal'. The vitality of this Rotterdam approach received international acclaim; architecture and planning, however, suffered during negotiations, leading to the negative expression 'urban renewal architecture'. Among the first realized projects are the stacked maisonettes with semi-circular staircases on Diergaardesingel and Gouvernestraat by Studio 8. Pietro Hammel's De Boogjes project consists of four blocks on Nieuwe Binnenweg and small, pedestrianized side streets lined by houses with gardens. The distinctive arches were a casualty of a renovation by Mecanoo Architects.

The Giant of Rotterdam

That was the nickname of Rigardus Rijnhout (1922-1959), the biggest man in the world at a height of 2.37 metres, shoe size 62 and a weight of 230 kilos. His growth was due to an over-active pituitary gland. Rijnhout lived at Gouvernestraat 3a. You can now literally tread in his footsteps in the nearby Oude Westen park, where a statue of the giant was erected in 2011.

8   Water Project

Westersingel, Spoorsingel,
Noordsingel, Crooswijksesingel,
Boezemsingel
W.N. Rose, J.A. Scholten Hzn.,
J.D. Zocher jr.
1854-
G.J. de Jongh (ext. Provenierssingel
(1896) and Bergsingel (1903)

Town Architect Willem Rose had made Rotterdam's water management the focus of his attention since 1840. In 1841 he designed together with works surveyor Jan Arent Scholten an initial version of his Water Project, followed in 1854 by the final version after a fresh outbreak of cholera. This was to be a network of singels, gently winding watercourses accompanied by a tree-lined avenue, as much a hygienic solution for flushing the town waters as a framework for urban expansion in the future. Designed in landscape style by the family firm of Zocher, these singels - Westersingel, Spoorsingel, Noordsingel, Crooswijksesingel and Boezemsingel - were the city's first public green facilities. To these Director of Public Works G.J. de Jongh would later add Provenierssingel and Bergsingel. The early twentieth-century Heemraadssingel is of a similar format. The mansions lining the singels were built between 1870 and 1900. In 2000, the Westersingel was renovated and partially paved to create a sculpture terrace.

Sculpture terrace

In 2000 Westersingel was renovated and part of it hard-surfaced as a sculpture terrace bringing together a number of pieces initially scattered across the city: Umberto Mastroianni's The Farewell from the old Central Station, Fritz Wotruba's Reclining Figure, Auguste Rodin's L'Homme Qui Marche **A5** and Henri Laurens' La Grande Musicienne. They were joined by more recent sculptures by Joel Shapiro and Carel Visser. Already during the Sculpture in the City event of 1988, the 'cultural axis' from Central Station to Veerhaven harbour basin did duty as a sculpture route. A remnant of this is The Long, Thin, Yellow Legs of Architecture, courtesy of Coop Himmelb(l)au **A12** at the corner of Vasteland.

Kruisplein 200-1048
Alsop Architects
2003-2013
Van der Laan Bouma (assoc.)

The site occupied during the post-war reconstruction period by the Rijnhotel, the Calypso Cinema and the Pauluskerk, is now home to the Calypso apartment complex. The irregularly shaped complex comprises over 400 apartments, retail and restaurant spaces on the ground floor, 5000 m² of office space in the podium, and a car park. It consists of two sections: a discrete, 22 storey tower with red facade panels, and a long section of 18, 22 and 14 storeys faced with grey panels. The angular facade shapes are not picked up in the interior and the apartments, too, have 'normal' floor plans. A much smaller Pauluskerk, imagined as a crystal that has broken off from the craggy complex, returns as a blob-like, copper clad semi-detached building.

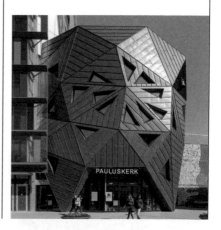

Rotjeknor, city of nicknames

The people of Rotterdam love giving the city's buildings nicknames. The new Pauluskerk for example has been variously dubbed 'doughnut', 'burning sun' and 'diamond'.

Other nicknames included Quist's Box (Schouwburg, **11d**), The Tub (Feijenoord Stadium, **94**), The Swan (Erasmus Bridge, **70**), The Pencil (Piet Blom Tower Block, **28**), Spendthrift Gully (Beurstraverse, **14**), Hookers' Walk (Rijnhavenbrug), The Aubergine (Coolse Poort office building), The Glass Palace (Van Nelle Factory, **52**), The Lightning Bolt (DWL District apartment block, **67**), The Hef (Hefbrug, **71**), The Banana (Het Nieuwe Instituut Collections Building, **31**), The High Harlots (a phonetic play on the Hoge Heren, **38**).

'A more outra-geous disfigure-ment of a street front is in my view inconceivable.'

J. Verheul, 1925

Mauritsweg 35
J.J.P. Oud
1924-1925
Reconstruction 1986

In 1924 J.J.P. Oud designed the facade of Café De Unie on Coolsingel. In the subdivision of its surface and use of primary colours De Unie is a typical product of De Stijl. The modernist facade with its bright colours and gaudy advertisements contrasted starkly with the existing buildings and was roundly criticized. Lettering and illuminated signs are used architecturally to fulfil the facade's most important function, namely to attract attention. The decorative and therefore apparently anti-functionalist facade really does seem the most appropriate solution. De Unie was destroyed during the 1940 bombardment, the facade being reconstructed at this new site in 1986. After a period during which the space behind the facade housed a combination of culture and catering, in 2014 it reverted to a purely catering function.

Site office

The temporary site office erected during the construction of the equally temporary Oud-Mathenesse housing estate is also a reconstruction. The shed consists of three interlocking volumes, each with its own colour. Oud made use both inside and out of the decorative properties of wood. For a time it served as a neighbourhood shop but during the war the dilapidated little building ended up as firewood. After Oud's White Village was pulled down and rebuilt in 1989 at Aakstraat 8, a replica of the works office building was built alongside it.

Fire line and reconstruction

*On 14 May 1940, urban renewal in Rotterdam was tackled
in a most radical way. Dorniers and Heinkels above the city.
Wham! Bang! Crack! In one fell swoop, the entire city was
razed to the ground.*

J.A. Deelder, Die stad komt nooit af, 1984

The 14th of May 1940 is a date Rotterdam will never forget.
Around one-thirty in the afternoon German bombers carried
out a raid on the historical city centre with the aim of forcing
a breakthrough in the German Blitzkrieg, which had stalled
at bridges over the River Maas. The bombardment lasted no
more than fifteen minutes, but the consequences were devas-
tating. Partly as a result of the ensuing fires, some 850 people
died and more than 24,000 dwellings were destroyed; around
80,000 Rotterdammers were made homeless. After the rubble
had been cleared away and the remains of damaged buildings
demolished, all that was left of the historic centre was a bare
expanse in which just a few buildings were left standing, including the city hall **15** and the post office **16**.

It is still possible to distinguish the 'fire line' (outer limits
of the conflagration) in the difference between the old, mainly
nineteenth-century buildings and the new, post-war construction. In 2010, in a design by Adriaan Geuze, this fire line was
marked for all time with a line of red lights in the pavement.

Notwithstanding the chaos, the city architect W.G. Witteveen embarked on a reconstruction plan just four days after the disaster. A crucial decision was taken to expropriate the entire area so as to be able to completely reorganize the centre where necessary and in particular to be able to tackle major pre-war bottlenecks like Hofplein and the slums around Goudsesingel. Nonetheless, in December 1941 Witteveen presented a plan based largely on the reconstruction of the historical urban structure. Even the proposed architecture referred to the pre-existing situation. Initially hampered by a lack of building materials, reconstruction stalled completely with the freeze on construction imposed in 1942. The longer the war lasted the more Witteveen's ideas came under fire. In 1944 the disillusioned city architect resigned, to be replaced by Cornelis van Traa. The reconstruction tide turned leaving the way clear for a completely new city centre.

Van Traa's Basic Plan for Reconstruction represented a radical break with the past. It was first and foremost an efficient traffic plan on an orthogonal grid. The Hofplein issue was resolved with a new roundabout; openings in Blaak and Mariniersweg made for an improved throughflow of traffic. In line with modernist urban planning ideas, a separation of functions was imposed, with priority being given to commercial buildings, public buildings and shops in the centre. Housing scarcely got a look-in. In the early reconstruction years the repair of the docks and the construction of multi-company buildings took precedence. Because many public-oriented uses, such as the Groothandelsgebouw ◨ and the Lijnbaan shopping precinct ◓, were located on the west side of Coolsingel, the heart of the city shifted accordingly. The Basic Plan continued to govern spatial policy in the centre until 1970. At that point criticism of the emptiness, the lack of dwellings and more especially of 'conviviality' started to gain the upper hand and a process of consolidation of the centre was set in train, although the traffic plan remained unaltered.

It'll be beautiful, Rotterdam will become a beautiful city. Rotterdam will be spacious, it will exude metropolitan allure: the fast-moving traffic, the wide boulevards, the tall buildings will together create an atmosphere of hustle and bustle in keeping with modern life. It won't be cosy, but right now we'd rather see a line of shiny automobiles than a carriage with elderly ladies and we feel more at home in a retail store of glass and mirrors than in an old-fashioned grocer's shop, where our sense are pleasantly assaulted by the aroma of cloves, soap and candy. Rotterdam will be our city, the city of twentieth-century man.

Rein Blijstra in Het Vrije Volk, 12 November 1952

11ª Schouwburgplein

Schouwburgplein
A.H. Geuze (West 8)
1990-1997

For many years, the open space between the theatre **11d** and the concert hall **11b** had been one the post-war city's most challenging urban design problems. In 1990 the City of Rotterdam accepted a proposal by landscape architect Adriaan Geuze for the redesign of Schouwburgplein. In it the 'theatre square' is conceived as a podium raised 35 cm above street level; the lighting installed in this space gives an effect of floating. The square is divided into three functional zones each with its own type of paving. The largest, central zone is finished in light metal so as to support more robust activity. The one to the east of wood and rubber is a gathering space complete with pavement cafés and lit by four hydraulic light masts. The third zone of poured concrete levelled with epoxy is largely in the shade. In 2010 a few modifications in the materials were carried out under West 8's supervision.

11ᵇ De Doelen

Schouwburgplein 50
E.H.A. & H.M.J.H. Kraaijvanger,
R.H. Fledderus
1955-1966
J. Hoogstad (ext. Codarts 1993-1999)

Rotterdam's concert hall has a square plan shared by a number of principal forms. Reacting against the business-like city centre, its appearance was intended as an expression of culture, hence the copper facing of the roof structure and more particularly the stone ornamental facade. This grid of beams and posts has not gone uncriticized; the structurally illogical facade suggests three storeys rather than the actual one or two. Jan Hoogstad's new additions along and above the concert hall house congress facilities and the combined Rotterdam Dance Academy and Conservatoire.

11ᶜ   Pathé Schouwburgplein

Schouwburgplein 101
K.J. van Velsen
1992-1996

This complex of seven cinema auditoria constructed as part of the reconstruction of the Schouwburgplein sits atop the existing parking facility, necessitating a building of the lightest construction. The structure is of steel and, apart from the steel plate reinforced concrete floor slabs, carries light materials such as gypsum board and corrugated sheet. Steel columns bear aloft four big auditoria above a large foyer zone beneath which are a further three smaller auditoria. By lifting up the big auditoria, so that the 'theatre square' continues on into the foyer, and stressing the deviating lines of the auditoria, the architect seeks to reduce the impression of bulk. Much of the building is wrapped in transparent corrugated sheet.

11ᵈ   City Theatre

Schouwburgplein 25
W.G. Quist
1982-1988

The tightest of budgets and an awkward site were the limiting conditions for this building which replaced the post-war temporary theatre. The 34 metre tall fly tower had to be placed at the front to allow light into the housing beyond. The plan has a symmetrical layout: from the entrance below the fly tower, long stately stairs lead past the auditorium to the foyer at the rear, an interesting spatial configuration of landings, galleries and voids. Quist's level-headedness and restraint dominate both inside and out, even in the grey and red main auditorium.

Lijnbaan, Korte Lijnbaan
Van den Broek & Bakema
1951-1953
Van den Broek & Bakema
(ext. 1962-1966)

In 1951, after much hesitation over the site and form of a new shopping precinct in the centre of the devastated city, Van den Broek & Bakema were commissioned to design 65 shops. These were built in two levels along two intersecting pedestrian streets. Unlike the traditional Dutch shopping street, dwellings and office space were not placed above the shops but behind them in separate blocks. The street profile, rather than being tall and narrow, is accordingly low and broad. The shops have a concrete frame, allowing for flexible subdivision of their interiors. Partition walls are of brick. As a rule one shop consist of two levels (above a basement), with three levels for staff at the back. All shops are 15 or 20 metres deep, but of varying width. The facades are built up of prefabricated concrete posts and panels using a basic module of 1.1 metres. Awnings composed of steel girders hung from the concrete frame and finished in varnished red deal, extend along the facades. Arcades at various points, kiosks, display cases, plant boxes and paving together model the pedestrian precinct. All shops take in stock from

a service road at their rear which also functions as an access road for the precinct's housing. This is contained in blocks of three, thirteen and nine storeys respectively, each enfolding a communal green space.

In 1966 the Lijnbaan was extended to Binnenwegplein, there to join up with another key shopping area dominated by two more retail buildings by Van den Broek & Bakema: H.H. de Klerk, and Ter Meulen/Wassen/Van Vorst ▮13. As the prototype of a traffic-free shop-

ping centre, the Lijnbaan has been imitated all over the world. Its unique urban layout of pedestrian precinct, service road and high-rise housing off courtyards has produced one of the few successful forms of urban dwelling, a form seemingly able to absorb without effort even the vast office slabs

of the 1970s. The flexible subdivision of shops, simple systematic architecture and thoughtfully shaped pedestrian street have managed to survive several generations of interior designers and shop decorators. Since the late 1980s the original concept has been subject to considerable depredation in the form of renovations and new, transparent awnings. In 2010 the Lijnbaan was accorded listed status and the architect Robert Winkel is currently in charge of an attempt to restore the original qualities.

'In planning the Lijnbaan, the architects have made a dramatic contribution to the modern city, for they have shown that the advantages we associate in America with the suburban or regional shopping center may also be made available in the heart of a metropolis.'

Lewis Mumford,
A Walk Through Rotterdam, 1957

13   Ter Meulen/The Karel Doorman

Binnenwegplein
Van den Broek & Bakema
1948-1951
Ibelings van Tilburg (ext. 2003-2012)

The Ter Meulen/Wassen/Van Vorst retail building originally comprised three quite separate shops: a department store, a ladies' clothes shop and a shoe store. This tripartition is visible in the facade, though the interior was one continuous space separated only by glass partitions. At the east end of this 100 metre long building are two entresols which project sculpture-like from the acute-angled corner of the facade. These cantilevers are suspended from the level above. In the facade, concrete beams 1.1 metres in height constitute a dominant visual element, with brick infills separated by glass strips. In 1976-77 the building was extended with a lateral wing to the Lijnbaan 🔟 and with an extra level, which was subsequently demolished to make way for the Karel Doorman project, a new, light roof structure comprising two 70 metre tall apartment towers by Ibelings van Tilburg. The roof of the shopping centre will be used as parking space for the apartments.

Snack bar architecture

This permanent snack bar for Bram Ladage, Rotterdam's best-known mobile purveyor of French fries consists of a six-metre-high coke can and a stainless steel awning above the sales and frying area. The roof, which juts a full five metres, is held aloft by two posts. Architects Kees Christiaanse and Chiel van der Stelt were inspired by American diners. The can, a Pop-Art artefact à la Claes Oldenburg in itself, contains a space for storage, a toilet plus hand washing facilities and the extract system. At night when the snack bar closes, a 15-metre-long horizontal roller shutter seals off the sales counter.

Beurstraverse
P.B. de Bruijn, The Jerde Partnership
1991-1996

This sunken pedestrian mall, almost immediately dubbed the 'Koopgoot' ('Spendthrift Gully' comes close), links two major shopping streets, Hoogstraat **22** and Lijnbaan **12**, via Beursplein metro station. One effect is to reduce the increased number of pedestrians crossing Coolsingel. The walls of this 'tunnel' resemble Italian arcades and consist entirely of small shops. Two winding canopies are meant to stress the unity of the shopping centre. The original post-war reconstruction architecture on site has been replaced by a metropolitan centre of 'contemporary' design topped off by a residential tower block.

'What's more, the meandering cutting of the Beurstraverse is a welcome relief in a Dutch city where everything else is strictly orthogonal: an anti-Lijnbaan which does not however render that famous post-war shopping street obsolete, but actually complements it architecturally and is one of the best arguments for preserving that same Lijnbaan.'

Angelika Schnell, Rotterdam Herzien, 2007

15   City Hall

Coolsingel 40
H.J. Evers
1912-1920

The City Hall and the post office **16**
were built when the waters of
Coolsingel were exchanged for a road
and 't Zand (the red light district) was
demolished. In 1913 a limited entry
competition among seven architects
to design a city hall was won by the
neo-Renaissance submission by Henri
Evers, who had in fact organized the
competition. The building comprises
four wings four storeys high about a
public court; the overall shape is a rec-
tangle of 86 x 106 metres. Presiding
over the City Hall is a 71 metre high
tower in reinforced concrete above
the main lobby. The building's exterior is dominated by the sandstone of
the elevations and the tall pyramidal
slate roofs. During a refurbishment
carried out between 2008 and 2010,
many rooms were restored to their
former glory; the attics beneath the
tall roofs, previously used for storage,
were turned into meeting rooms and a
restaurant.

Oasis of peace

Running right through the town hall is a
street through which cars carrying digni-
taries and carriages with bridal couples
can reach the rear entrance without
getting wet. Here, too, is the town hall
garden, an oasis of peace in the very heart
of the city. In the centre of the garden
stands a fountain donated by the Maas
towns of Schiedam, Vlaardingen and
Maassluis; two seated bronze figures by
sculptor Jan Ingen-Housz portray Mercury
and Neptune. A large terracotta frieze
above the gallery beneath the council
chamber depicts the five key departments
of municipal administration: Education,
Finance, Poor Relief, Public Works and
Business.

16 Main Post Office

Coolsingel 42
G.C. Bremer
1915-1923
J.P.H. van Lunteren (artist)

Designed by the Government Architect G.C. Bremer, the post office is set back ten metres from the building line of the City Hall **15** as a sign of deference. This did gain it a forecourt, which in fact produced quite the opposite effect. Its subdued neoclassical appearance conceals a surprisingly airy interior, a large 22.5 metre high hall set widthways in the building below a concrete parabolic barrel vault with skylights and coffering. Outside, the four shell-limestone elevations reach up four storeys to terminate in a mansard roof. The post office was decommissioned in 2007; there are plans to convert the building into a shopping centre and hotel.

Coolsingel pavilions

During the C70 event (in 1970), the city centre was transformed into one big exhibition site, the highlight being a cable-car route through the centre. At the time there was a lot of criticism of the lack of conviviality in the centre, so after the event many of the pavilions built along the wide Coolsingel boulevard remained in place. Over time, however, they disappeared again. It seems you can have too much conviviality. Nevertheless, new pavilions have been built and in 2015 the old McDonalds Pavilion was actually rebuilt by the architect Robert Winkel.

Coolsingel 105
M. Breuer, A. Elzas
1955-1957
N. Gabo (artist)

Unlike the former Bijenkorf ('Beehive')
designed by W.M. Dudok but later
demolished in the aftermath of the
wartime bombing raid, this post-war
version of the department store by the
Hungarian-American Bauhaus architect Marcel Breuer, was executed as
an almost completely sealed box.
A column grid of 12 metres ensures

an optimum subdivision of the sales
area. Front and rear elevations have
a honeycomb cladding of hexagonal
travertine panels with horizontal and
vertical fluting and slits of fenestration. The restaurant and offices have
larger windows. As Breuer refused to
conform to the double building line of
Coolsingel, a monumental sculpture
by Naum Gabo A4 was placed in front
of the Bijenkorf to compensate. In 2012
the 70 metre high B-Tower apartment
building by Wiel Arets was built on the
site of the Bijkorama.

Car park

Breuer's Bijenkorf is universally
acclaimed as one of the most handsome
buildings of the reconstruction period. So
which second-rate architect designed the
accompanying hideous car park? None
other than Marcel Breuer! In 1974 Breuer
attended a meeting of the design review
committee in person in order to defend
his design. At that point, no one dared to
reject a design that was the embodiment
of 'fifty years of experience in architecture'.

18 Stock Exchange; World Trade Center

Beursplein 37
J.F. Staal; R.B. van Erk, A.H. Veerbeek
(Groosman Partners)
1925-1940; 1983-1986

Staal received this commission by winning a competition in 1928 also entered by J.J.P. Oud. The ultimate design, however, deviates radically from the competition scheme. A slender bell-tower and a meeting hall on stilts mark the entrance. The exchange hall of 90 x 60 metres is spanned by arched steel girders clad in concrete panels embedded with round glazed tiles. A gently curving glass bay window gives a wide view of the Coolsingel boulevard. During renovations the café on the plaza (Beursplein) and the meeting room of the Chamber of Commerce were restored to their original state.

Standing above the hall of the Exchange parallel to Coolsingel is this 20-storey office block. Shaped like a flattened ellipse, it rests on a concrete table held aloft by eight columns, thus minimizing loss of space within the hall below. Its elliptical shape, green glazing and aluminium cladding panels stem from forms and colours in the original building beneath. The WTC proved to be the starting signal for a deluge of high-rises in the centre during the 1980s and '90s.

Etched against ever-changing skies
The green-sided World Trade Center
Towers above Rotterdam's Stock Exchange

A. Moonen

Culture

Most of Rotterdam's museums are located along the Leuvenhaven–Museumpark axis. Museum Boijmans Van Beuningen 33 on Museumpark is one of the top art museums in the Netherlands. It shows Dutch and European masterpieces from the Middle Ages to the twentieth century; from Bruegel, Rembrandt, Van Gogh, Mondrian and Dalí to contemporary Dutch Design. Also on Museumpark are Rem Koolhaas's Kunsthal 35, which combines art and popular culture in temporary exhibitions, Het Nieuwe Instituut 31 with exhibitions on architecture, design and fashion. Nearby these major drawcards are the Natural History Museum and the modest Chabot Museum, housed in characteristic Museumpark white villas. Museumpark feeds into Witte de Withstraat, which is lined by a combination of trendy cafés and restaurants and numerous small galleries as well as Witte de With, the centre for contemporary art, and TENT, a platform for local contemporary art.

Reflecting Rotterdam's port city status are the Maritime Museum 29 and the World Museum (Willemskade 25, see illustration), both originally based on objects from around the world collected by merchants and diplomats. Museum Rotterdam, for many years located in the Schielandshuis 19, has relocated to the new Timmerhuis 21. The museum's collection focuses on the city's past and present. One exception to the centralized location of Rotterdam's museums, is the Nederlands Fotomuseum, which is housed in Las Palmas 75 on Wilhelmapier.

Schouwburgplein 11 is flanked by Rotterdam's two historically most important cultural buildings, the Doelen concert hall and the Rotterdam Theatre. One of Pathé's two multiplex cinemas is also located here. LantarenVenster on Kop van Zuid 72 and Cinerama on Westblaak are the only remaining traditional cinemas in a city that once boasted 27 cinemas.
Rotterdam-Zuid acquired its own theatre in 1954 and in 1970 Ahoy', a multifunctional complex for sport, music, trade fairs and exhibitions, was built here. The two main theatres are the New Luxor (Kop van Zuid) and the Old Luxor (Kruiskade).

Pop music and jazz tend to be concentrated in smaller clubs like Rotown, Bird, Grounds and Walhalla. An important venue for alternative culture is WORM on Boomgaardsstraat. The interior is fashioned entirely from recycled material.

19 Schielandshuis

Korte Hoogstraat 31
J. Lois with P. Post
1662-1665
J. Toorn, P. Rijckx, H. Jansz (artists)

The Schielandshuis was designed by the Rotterdam linen merchant and historian Jacob Lois in association with the renowned architect Pieter Post. It was built in 1665 to domicile the Schieland Water Control Board, which had its origins in the 13th century. It was gutted by fire in 1864 and subsequently rebuilt. Alterations carried out in 1981-1985 were aimed at restoring the building as much as possible to its original state. The only surviving 17th-century building in the centre, the Schielandshuis has housed in succession the municipal archives, the Boijmans Museum **33**, the Academy of Fine Arts and the Rotterdam Historical Museum.

Napoleon Bonaparte

The members of the water control boards met four times a year in the Schielandshuis, dining and staying the night in the guest rooms. At 11 pm on Friday 25 April 1811 a special guest arrived via the Delftse Poort in Rotterdam: Napoleon Bonaparte. The Schielandshuis had been temporarily fitted out as an imperial palace. Napoleon and his wife Marie Louise dined and slept there. At 7 am on Sunday 27 October Napoleon left Rotterdam, donating 15,000 francs to the poor.

Meent 88
W.M. Dudok
1942-1952
(H.H.R. Kossmann, J.G.C. Dijkman,
int. des. 1991)

It was only in 1991, when a 'grand café' was opened in this former De Nederlanden insurance office from 1845, that this building by Dudok came into the public eye. The post-war work of this architect who trod the dividing line between traditionalism and functionalism is regarded as being of lesser significance, most probably without justification. The building combines a six metre high basement with four levels of maisonettes, the whole topped by a curved concrete shell roof. The ground floor is dominated by the six metre high staff hall with its large expanses of glass and enlivened only by round columns. The former entry zone on the Meent boasts a mezzanine.

Window on the river

A large part of another Dudok building, the pre-war Bijenkorf, escaped the bombardment only to be demolished under Cornelis van Traa's Basic Plan for Reconstruction in 1957. The striking glass building had to make way for the 'window on the river', a sightline from the city centre to the River Maas. Locals did not enjoy the view of the water for long, though. With the construction of the Maritime Museum 29 on virtually the same spot the window was closed again in 1986.

21 Timmerhuis

Rodezand
OMA
2009-2015
J.R.A. Koops (Public Works)
(Stadstimmerhuis 1947-1953)

In 2009 OMA won the commission for the redevelopment of the
old Stadstimmerhuis. The original
1953 municipal office on Meent and
Haagseveer, designed by municipal
architect J.R.A. Koops, was restored,
while a later extension on Rodezand
was demolished and replaced
by a mixed-use building containing shops, offices and apartments.
The extension comprises a 'floating
cloud' of glass cubes supported on
two steel feet, allowing the ground

floor space to be largely free of columns. This public space, containing
shops, municipal services as well as
Museum Rotterdam, is bisected by an
arcade that forms a new link between
Coolsingel and the Laurenskwartier.
The 'cloud' consists of a three-dimen-
sional Vierendeel steel structure, a
cubic grid of 7.2 by 7.2 metres. Within
this grid are apartments and offices.
The construction method allows the
building to cantilever up to 17 metres.
Parts of the fully glazed elevations are
printed with a pattern of dots. Thanks
to the stepped composition, the apartments enjoy spacious roof terraces.

Basic Plan

Set into the side elevation of the old
Stadstimmerhuis, on the corner of Meent
and Rodezand, is a plaque commemorat-
ing Cornelis van Traa (1899-1970),
the man behind the Basic Plan for
Reconstruction. The plaque, designed by
Cor van Kralingen, was unveiled in the
hall of the Stadstimmerhuis in 1971. 'The
reconstruction of Rotterdam was his life's
work in which he invested all his abilities
and knowledge, his intelligence and his
emotions,' recalled J.A.C. Tillema.

22 Huf Shoe Store

Hoogstraat 183
Van den Broek & Bakema
1952-1954
W. de Jonge (ren. 2010)

In the mid 1950s, the Huf shoe store, along with that other Van den Broek & Bakema designed retail outlet, Galeries Modernes, constituted a fine modern interpretation of the latest ideas on shopping. To conform to the urban design profile of Westewagenstraat an additional three storeys of office space were stacked on top of the fully glazed ground floor retail store. A caretaker's dwelling was added to the roof. Behind the concrete collar on the first floor lay the stockrooms. Prolonged neglect turned the Huf Building into a modern ruin, but since the restoration in 2009 the listed building is now almost more beautiful than ever.

Hoogstraat

Hoogstraat was once Rotterdam's oldest and most important shopping street. Although the many cinemas and nightspots did not return after the war, the shops – Hema, C&A, Huf and Galeries Modernes – did. The first section of Hoogstraat is lined by the more traditionalist stores of Peek & Cloppenburg, Lampe and Martens (Blokker), designed by the Kraaijvanger brothers. Near Binnenrotte was the dam in the River Rotte from which Rotterdam derives its name.

> 'I doubt you will find another statue of a man of letters that is so little remarked by passers-by, so marred by its surroundings and so lamented by those who pay it due regard.'

Edmondo de Amicis,
Olanda, 1874

Grotekerkplein 15
Architect unknown
1499-1525
J. Poot, J.C. Meischke (rest. 1952-1971);
W.G. Quist (ext. 1976-1981)

The St. Laurenskerk (or Grote Kerk) is the only built reminder of Rotterdam in the Middle Ages. The city's principal church, it was erected between 1449 and 1525, though its tower was increased in height several times until as late as 1645. A cruciform basilica in plan, it has a central aisle of six bays and two broad side aisles with small shallow chapels. A less-tall, narrower pentagonal ambulatory surrounds the choir. Facades are of brick, interspersed with bands of stone; piers and sundry decorations are of sandstone. The nave and the side aisles have a roof of wooden barrel vaults. Badly damaged in the Second World War, the church was restored between 1952 and 1970. The bronze doors, whose theme is War and Peace, were designed by Giacomo Manzù and installed in 1968. In 1991 the church was enlarged by Wim Quist with five black stone-clad cubes connected to each other by glass passages so as not to obscure the height of the church windows behind.

Desiderius Erasmus

One of Rotterdam's best-known sons is the humanist Desiderius Erasmus (c. 1466-1536), whose works include the famous satire In Praise of Folly. His name and likeness are ubiquitous in the city. In reality, the illegitimate son of a priest from Gouda left Rotterdam aged four, never to return. The bronze statue by the celebrated sculptor and architect Hendrick de Keyser from 1622 is the oldest statue in the Netherlands. Erasmus stands on a tall plinth, engrossed in a book and in the act of turning a page.

Wijnhaven 3/Geldersekade
W. Molenbroek
1897-1898
S. Miedema (artist)

Eleven storeys and 45 metres high, this office block was for a long time Europe's tallest office building. As this first Dutch 'skyscraper' has no skeleton but is built up of loadbearing walls (0.40-1.40 metres thick) criss-crossed by four less-heavy wall partitions for stability, first professional press reports were negative. Its facade, too, of glazed brick with mosaics and sculpture was dismissed as kitsch. Yet this building has become very popular in Rotterdam, partly due to the public viewing platform on the roof.

A Dutch skyscraper

'Holland has one too, and it's in the city of Rotterdam, which can pride itself on having the tallest building in Europe. Anyone who has ever been to the Maas city knows this Dutch skyscraper and many visitors yield to temptation and hand over a 25 cent piece for a trip in the lift up to the belvédère, in order to enjoy the magnificent panorama. You do not need to be afraid of falling off because the platform is surrounded on all sides by a railing. You are standing 43 metres above ground level, so that even with the naked eye you can see a very long way.'

J.M. Droogendijk, Voor 't Jonge Volkje, 1918

Ds. Jan Scharpstraat 298, Westnieuwland
MVRDV
2004-2014
A. Coenen, I. Roskam (artists)

In 2014, Rotterdam suddenly started to feature in various international lists of 'places to visit'. This city marketing coup was due in part to the completion of this spectacular combination of covered market and housing. The horseshoe shaped building mass contains 200 apartments, each with a window overlooking the market. On the ground floor of the horseshoe are shops and restaurants. The arch covers a public space of 120 x 70 metres and a height of 40 metres. Permanent 'market stalls', whose roofs are also accessible, are set out on a square grid. Both end facades are entirely of glass, supported by a network of steel tension cables. The remaining elevations and the floor of the hall are clad in grey stone. Below ground are a large supermarket and 1200 parking spaces. The entire inner face of the Markthal is covered with Horn of Plenty, an 11,000 m² artwork by Arno Coenen and Iris Roskam, which depicts the products on sale below in a greatly magnified form.

Collection of architectural curiosities along Binnenrotte

Telephone Company Building, J.R.A. Koops (Public Works), 1940-1951
Central Library, Van den Broek & Bakema, 1977-1983
Blaakse Bos **26**, P. Blom, 1978-1984
Station Blaak, H.C.H. Reijnders, 1987-1993
Housing Block City Building, J. Bosch, 1998-2003
Housing Block De Hofdame, Klunder Architects, 2003-2007
Housing Block Statendam, H.F. Kollhoff, 2000-2009
Office Building Laurenshof, Rapp + Rapp, 2004-2009
Office Building Blaak 31, KCAP, 2007-2010
Office Building Blaak 8, Group A, Dreissen Architects, 2004-2011
Hotel CitizenM Oude Haven, ZZDP Architects with Concrete, 2001-2014

Blaak, Spaansekade
P. Blom
1978-1984

The Amsterdam architect Piet Blom spent years working on his concept of an 'urban roof' of housing with the Kasbah in Hengelo (1973) and cube houses in Helmond (1976). The third manifestation of this theory, Blaakse Bos (Blaak Woods), is part of a plan for Oudehaven. Blom felt that this former harbour area's only chance of success would be if it were to be linked to the market and the central library by a Ponte Vecchio-type pedestrian bridge across Blaak and its traffic. Only 38 of the projected 74 cube houses were built. A residential tower, the 'Pencil', was built to compensate. The development on Oudehaven itself combines 250 social housing units with cafés and restaurants along the dockside walkway. The whole has a high structural density and a 'Mediterranean' vernacular and, being ideally oriented to the sun, it has burgeoned into a popular leisure zone for tourists and students. One of the two large cubes has been occupied since 2009 by a Stayokay hostel; the other, since 2013, by a sheltered housing project. In late 2013, the area around Oudehaven was finally completed with the construction of an office building plus CitizenM hotel above the railway tunnel (ZZDP Architects with Concrete).

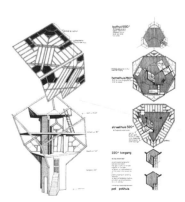

Museum cube house

Cube houses, also known as pole or tree dwellings, consist of a tilted timber cube with one point anchored in a hexagonal concrete core. This 'trunk' contains the entrance and the stair. The cube itself has three levels: a 'street-house' of kitchen and living room, a 'sky-house' of bedrooms and a 'tree-top-house' at the apex. The only vertical walls are in the core; all the others are at an angle. In the Museum Cube House, Overblaak 70, open daily from 11 am to 5 pm, people can see and judge for themselves.

27   The Red Apple

Wijnbrugstraat 50-350/Wijnhaven
H.G.J. van den Born (KCAP)
2002-2009

Kees Christiaanse's urban strategy for the Wijnhaveneiland lays down the rules of play for developing the area. These include retaining intact the post-war structure of blocks to a height of 20 metres. Above that, there is a restricted available volume of 35 cubic metres per square metre of owned land, the only option being slim-line high-rise. The first buildings to arrive on site are HM Architects' three Waterstadtorens (Harbour Village apartment towers) and Taco Pino's Scheepmakerstoren.

The newest project is 100hoog by Klunder Architects. Christiaanse's KCAP is also responsible for The Red Apple. This housing block of 231 units at the point where Wijnhaven meets Scheepmakershaven combines a slender tower 120 metres tall and a low cantilevering wedge of housing round an atrium. Both stand on a 'plinth' of shops, office space and indoor parking. Anodized aluminium bars rising up the tower's exterior narrow as the view becomes more spectacular. Units have full-height glazing and French balconies.

Architects' quarter

Both before and after the Second World War, most Rotterdam architects were located in this part of Rotterdam, known as Waterstad: Barend Hooijkaas, Willem Kromhout, Brinkman & Van der Vlugt, Van Tijen & Maaskant, Van den Broek & Bakema (Posthoornstraat 12), EGM, DSBV, Hoogstad and OMA (Boompjes 55-57). Willem Molenbroek moved into an office in his own creation, Het Witte Huis 24, in 1898. For a short time in the late 1930s the Haarlem architect J.B. van Loghem rented office space here as well.

28 Willemswerf

Boompjes 40
W.G. Quist
1983-1989

Occupying an impossible sliver of urban leftover space are these 16 levels of offices above a five-storey car park. Rising above the understructure with its free-standing double screw-shaped car park entrance is a rectangular slab with tiled concrete panels and a wedge-shaped curtain wall. Two L-shaped concrete piers in the rear elevation ensure stability and contain vertical circulation. The road at the rear runs beneath the building. The glass wedge was the setting for the spectacular finale of the Jackie Chan film, *Who Am I*.

The city as decor

'Rotterdam can't be filmed, Rotterdam's much too real', is a famous line from Jules Deelder's poem Rotown Magic. Nonetheless, Rotterdam has provided the decor for many films, including De Marathon (2012), Who Am I (1998), Loos (1989), A Zed and Two Noughts (1985), Spetters (1980), Chinese Kung Fu against Godfather (1973), Boefje (1939) and The Bridge (1928). Films of novels set in pre-war Rotterdam are usually filmed elsewhere: in Wroclaw (Karakter, 1997), Ghent and Bruges (Pietje Bell, 2002) or Budapest (Het Bombardement, 2012).

Shopping

After the reconstruction period, shopping in Rotterdam started up in the new centre: on the Lijnbaan ⑫ and around Coolsingel and Beursplein, where the major chain stores and department stores are located. Lijnbaan and Hoogstraat, the main pre-war shopping streets, are linked by the sunken Beurstraverse, popularly known as the Koopgoot (Spendthrift Gully) ⑭. Close by is Kruiskade with exclusive clothing stores, and Meent, Van Oldenbarneveltstraat and Witte de Withstraat with trendier shops and cafés. Pannekoekstraat, Nieuwemarkt and the second section of Hoogstraat are also on the rise. One unusual example of the vitality of reconstruction architecture is Groene Passage, a people- and environmentally-friendly shopping centre. Concrete, steel and glass provide an excellent decor for the world of free-range meat, herbal teas and yoga.

Anyone looking for something a bit different from the ubiquitous retail chains would do well to wander into one of the side streets in the centre. The further away from the centre, the more exotic and cheaper the goods. Running west from Binnenwegplein is an over three kilometre long shopping route lined by vinyl shops, pop-up stores, trendy clothes shops, hairdressers, breakfast bars and vintage clothing outlets. A similar route, offering exotic products, fabrics and clothing from around the world, begins in Rotterdam's multicultural 'Chinatown' at the end of West-Kruiskade.

The neighbourhoods around the centre still boast major shopping streets such as Oudedijk in Kralingen, Zwaanshals, Zwart Janstraat and Bergweg in Noord, and Beijerlandselaan in Zuid. The region's first covered shopping centre, Zuidplein, was built in Rotterdam-Zuid in 1972. There are megastores in Alexandrium and near Rooftop Park ㊽.

Rotterdam has long been famous for its many open-air markets. On Afrikaanderplein (Wednesday and Saturday) and Visserijplein (Thursday and Saturday) exotic products dominate. With 465 stalls, the central market on Binnenrotte (Tuesday and Saturday) is the largest in the country. In 2014 the Markthal ㉕ opened here, a new concept that is a cross between open-air market, department store and shopping centre; it drew millions of visitors in its first few months alone. Launched in 2010, the Swan Market is a lifestyle market packed with creative products, held on alternating locations. Feniksloods on Katendrecht ㉟ is home to the artisanal fresh-food outlet, Fenix Food Factory. For architecture and design enthusiasts there is only one really indispensable shop: NAi Booksellers in the foyer of Het Nieuwe Instituut ㉛.

Leuvehaven 1
W.G. Quist
1981-1986

This museum is situated at one of the town's key points, where two major boulevards meet at Leuvehaven. Its basic structure is one half of a square bisected along the diagonal with its oblique side towards the harbour. Half tucked in under this side is a double-height exhibition area. Steel ramps lead to an upper level containing exhibition spaces, a library and a roof terrace overlooking the harbour. In 2004 the museum was enlarged, keeping to its original style. In 2010 the entrance lobby was radically changed.

'Rotterdam possesses a certain ugliness that is an interesting phenomenon in architecture. In a context of ugliness, the most beautiful things can emerge.'

Reinier de Graaf (OMA), 2010

Destroyed City

The Destroyed City **A1** by the French-Russian sculptor Ossip Zadkine is without doubt the best-known and most cherished symbol of the havoc wreaked by the bombardment of May 1940. The bronze statue, a figure without a heart, was unveiled on Plein 1940 on 15 May 1953. The statue was a gift from the board of the Bijenkorf **17** department store, with the proviso that the statue would never be moved, a fate that did in fact befall many other statues in the city.

30 Live/work Building Kühne

Boomgaardsstraat 34
Kühne & Co
2007-2009

The Rotterdam architect Joost Kühne specializes in building on impossible locations and hidden spots in the city. In Boomgaardsstraat, on the border between the old and new city, he conjured an office-cum-home from an unpromising plot surrounded by car parks and the large-scale office buildings of Westblaak. Only by purchasing the air rights was it possible to build this 'floating' structure, consisting of a base containing the entrance, topped by a 54 metre long and a mere five metre deep section. The rear elevation abuts a parking garage and is completely imperforate; the street-facing front elevation is almost entirely of glass. Right at the top is a spacious apartment with roof terrace. Kühne has built dwellings on two other postage-stamp sites: Boomgaardhof 73 and Prins Hendrikkade 57.

Skate park

Rotterdam is a skateboarding city par excellence. Skaters don't like picturesque little streets paved with clinkers or cobblestones, preferring shiny smooth asphalt. Facilities for skaters are usually hidden away in outer suburbs or sports halls, but in Rotterdam a skate ramp was built in the middle of the city, on the central reservation of Westblaak. In 2015 the stainless steel ramps and half pipes were replaced by concrete objects, designed by Janne Saario.

Museumpark 25
J.M.J. Coenen
1988-1993
P. Struycken, A. de Vries,
L. Woods (artists)

When an invited competition for the Netherlands Architecture Institute building was held among six architects in 1988, Rem Koolhaas (OMA) was the hot favourite, but Jo Coenen the surprise winner. Coenen's design houses the institute's key functions - archives, exhibitions and staff - in three distinct volumes. Each volume has its own architectural character and relationship with the surroundings. The elongated archives building follows the curve of Rochussenstraat, screening off Museum Park from the rest of the city. It stands on concrete piers in a colonnade so that the park can be visually engaged through it. In the evening the colonnade plays host to Peter Struycken's spectacular light work. The exhibition block is a square concrete volume clad in brick. Besides the tall main exhibition space it contains two smaller rooms, a gallery and a Balcony Room. Exhibitions can also be held in the Upper or Attic Room between the six storey-high concrete joists; the floors there are of steel gratings through which daylight passes from the transparent roof down to the main exhibition space below. The tall central glass box contains offices and a library connected to the study areas in the archive block by a footbridge. The structure of this wing consists of steel columns on the exterior of the envelope that meet above the glass box in a steel 'pergola'. The central entrance lobby and foyer are situated in the base, giving access to the glazed auditorium overlooking the ornamental lake. The sculpture in the water is by Auke de Vries. In 2004 The Hermitage A14, a zinc and steel installation by Lebbeus Woods, was mounted on the north-east corner of the archives building. In 2011, Jo Coenen & Co oversaw a refurbishment that introduced a new entrance zone with restaurant and a DIY corner for children.
In 2013 the Netherlands Architecture Institute merged with the Netherlands Institute for Design and Fashion and the Virtual Platform to form Het Nieuwe Instituut, which focuses on architecture, design and e-culture.

32 Sonneveld House

Jongkindstraat 12
Brinkman & Van der Vlugt
1929-1933
Molenaar & Van Winden (rest. 1999-2001)

This steel-framed villa was intended for one of the directors of the Van Nelle Factory **52**. It consists of a tiled basement of services with a studio on the south side, living space on the first floor with a strip of fenestration the entire length of the facade, and bedrooms on the second. Like all Van der Vlugt's villas, it has a roof terrace. In 1997 the Sonneveld House with its array of innovations for home comfort was bought by the VHM foundation for historic monuments and restored in every detail as a museum house managed by Het Nieuwe Instituut **31**. Other white villas in Museumpark are: no. 7 Private House Merkes (J.F. van Teeffelen, 1932-1934), no. 9 Private House Boevé (Brinkman & Van der Vlugt, 1932-1934 and no. 11 Private House Kraayeveld (G.W. Baas, L. Stokla, 1938-1939), in use as the Chabot Museum. Van der Vlugt also designed the house at Kralingse Plaslaan 38 for Kees van der Leeuw, who commissioned the Van Nelle Factory.

'Even as a young boy I realized that this was a special house. My friends' homes were filled with oak furniture and Persian carpets, in our home there was light and space.'

Leonard Kooy, Sonneveld's grandson, Trouw, 24 February 1999

33 Boijmans Van Beuningen Museum

☕ 🍴 🏛

Museumpark 18
A. van der Steur
1928-1935
A. Bodon (DSBV) (ext. 1963-1972); H.A.J. Henket (Tuinpaviljoen 1989-1991); P. Robbrecht, H. Daem (ext. 1996-2003)

The traditional, Scandinavian inspired museum was designed by Rotterdam's City Architect, A. van der Steur. Two levels of exhibition galleries are grouped around a courtyard; applied arts on the ground floor behind a sandstone front, and painting upstairs with a facade incorporating two sizes of brick 'for the sake of enlivenment'. The tower was added for aesthetic reasons and contains storage space. This building, traditional, of Scandinavian influence yet functional in plan, was roundly criticized by the functionalist architects of the Nieuwe Bouwen. In 1972 the museum was extended with a large flexible exhibition wing designed by Alexander Bodon. On the garden side of the museum, an open, glass pavilion designed by Hubert-Jan Henket in 1991, contrasts with the introverted brick elevations of the existing building. The demolition of a villa on Westersingel enabled the Boijmans Van Beuningen Museum in 2003 to realize another extension by the Belgian architects Robbrecht and Daem. Behind the museum is the Museum Garden with a memorial to G.J. de Jongh. In the courtyard one can find an original call box designed by Brinkman & Van der Vlugt.

Call box

At the beginning of the 1930s J.F. van Royen, head of the Dutch postal service's Department of Art and Design, approached the architects Brinkman & Van der Vlugt about designing a public call box. Its design had to have something typically Dutch about it. The result was a transparent pillar of steel and glass with the telephone itself hung on two vertical steel posts. Produced by the firm of Gispen, the call box has the word 'telefoon' emblazoned on it in sanserif type. During its 50-year stint, 7500 examples of this call box were in operation all over the Netherlands.

Wytemaweg, Dr. Molewaterplein 40
J.L.C. Choisy, A. Hagoort, G.Th.J. Martens
(OD205)
1965-1968
OD205 (Sophia Kinderziekenhuis, 1987-
1994); EGM (ext. 2005-2018); Claus &
Kaan (ren. Education Centre 2006-2012)

The 114 metre high colossus of
the Medical Faculty dominated
Rotterdam's skyline from day one.
The high-rise slab contains laboratories, the low-rise block lecture halls
and administration. Its concrete frame
is fully clad in white enamelled aluminium sandwich panels designed by
Jean Prouvé. It was built in a remark-
ably short time by following flexible
standard plans and using extensive

prefabrication. The Medical Faculty
was an extension of the Dijkzigt
Hospital. Between 2005 and 2018,
the complex will be renovated and
rebadged as the Erasmus Medical
Centre, with 300,000 m² of parking
for 3000 cars. The overall design is by
EGM Architects with individual elements being developed by several different architects. From the outside,
the new education centre by Claus &
Kaan in the eastern low-rise wing –
library, study centre and central meeting place for students – is relatively
inconspicuous.

White

For decades the tall Medical Faculty building was a beacon sig-
nalling the city from a long way off; the dazzling white facades
could be seen from the motorway from The Hague. That bright
whiteness was due to the innovative facade panels employed.
These white enamelled aluminium sandwich panels were
designed by the French architect, furniture maker and industrial
designer, Jean Prouvé (1901-1984). Prouvé was a pioneer in the
field of industrially fabricated architecture.

Eating and drinking

Prior to the bombardment Rotterdam, like all port cities, had a vibrant entertainment district. Today's city still boasts a diverse entertainment scene, although you need to know where to find it.

Cafés, restaurants and terraces can be found all over the city, but are particularly numerous along Witte de Withstraat, around Oudehaven **26**, on Stadhuisplein, around the intersections of Nieuwe Binnenweg with 's-Gravendijkwal and Mathenesserlaan, in historic Delfshaven and along most shopping streets. For an ice cream go to Capri, Venezia, Angelo Betti or De IJssalon. The one-time red light district around Deliplein on Katendrecht **85** has metamorphosed into a new nightlife zone, while new cafés and restaurants can also be found in and around Schieblock **5** and Hofbogen **51**.

If you're looking for the best views of the River Maas, the terrace of Hotel New York **73** has long been top of the bill. Or you could combine lunch with a view of the entire city from the Euromast **41** or the terrace of Nhow in De Rotterdam **78**. And when the weather's fine the roof terrace of the Groothandelsgebouw **2** is open. Some time ago the former indoor leisure pool Tropicana morphed into a mushroom farm and cultural centre, including the Alohabar from where there is a superb view of the river. And to see the city from river, you could jump aboard a water taxi or take a short cruise with the Spido.

Restaurants, ranging from Michelin star quality to non-traditional fast-food outlets, are also scattered across the city. They are particularly thick on the ground on Witte de Withstraat and the area around Veerhaven. Close by is the Westelijk Handelsterrein **36**, a 'mall' of restaurants and galleries. Rotterdam's multicultural make-up is reflected in a profusion of Chinese and Indonesian restaurants, Turkish and Moroccan eateries and Surinamese takeaways, especially in the working-class districts and around Kruisplein and West-Kruiskade.

A new development on the culinary front is the gourmet burger bar, such as Ter Marsch, Hamburg, Ellis Gourmet Burger and Burgertrut. Meanwhile, under the label 'Haute Friture', the local snack bar culture is undergoing a veritable organic revival courtesy of new players like Fritez, Tante Nel and Pomms'. But if it's a genuine Rotterdam snack you're after, you should order a 'kapsalon' (literally 'hair salon'), an adventurous combination of chips, spicy meat and sauces, rounded off with a layer of melted Gouda cheese and topped with salad.

Westzeedijk 341
R.L. Koolhaas, F. Hoshino (OMA)
1988-1992
H. Visch (artist)

The Kunsthal is intended as a show-case for temporary exhibitions which cannot be accommodated at existing venues. Abutting on the dyke embankment of Westzeedijk, it is transected by a pedestrian route from Museumpark to Westzeedijk and a service road at the foot of the dyke. The building itself is in fact one huge traffic zone, a spiralling system of ramps around the pedestrian route which is itself a ramp. This route slices the building into two portions: a broad wing on the east side containing two large exhibition rooms and a narrower zone on the west housing the auditorium, once again a single large ramp, with a café-restaurant below and a third, smaller exhibition room above.

The two large galleries differ in character. The one on the ground plane is a continuation of the park, with black painted ceiling and walls, irregular lighting patterns and four steel columns dressed as tree trunks. The other is a large column-free space two floors up with a transparent roof and a big display window looking out on the busy road atop the dyke. Travertine and tarred concrete alternate with large expanses of glass in the facades, each of which is a self-sufficient unit. The one looking onto Westzeedijk acts as a display window, with a services tower on the roof functioning as a billboard to advertise the exhibitions inside. In the Kunsthal materials and constructional elements have been spliced together with no attempt at reconciliation. Contrasting materials, cheap and expensive, elegant and banal, are brazenly juxtaposed. The Museumpark ⑥⑦ is designed to a plan by the French landscape architect Yves Brunier in association with OMA. The area divides into four zones: a museum zone containing the Kunsthal and the Natural History Museum, a romantic garden, a raised multi-purpose area in black asphalt and a forecourt.

Natural History Museum

Villa Dijkzigt, a neoclassical design by J.F. Metzelaar from 1850, was once the home of Anthony van Hoboken. Since 1995 it has housed the Natural History Museum, for which Erick van Egeraat designed an extension in the form of a freestanding, orthogonal glass pavilion. Air bridges connect the pavilion to the villa.

Van Vollenhovenstraat 15
Th.L. Kanters
1894
H. Klunder, J.W. van der Weerd
(ren. 1999-2001)

Behind the stately facades of the Scheepvaartkwartier ('Maritime Quarter') lies Westelijk Handelsterrein, a 19th-century complex of split-level warehouses with grass roofs. The 36 storage depots are six metres wide with a depth of 25 metres on the left-hand side and almost 40 metres on the right-hand side. These were reached through a gateway, later modified to accommodate lorries. It was the brainchild of J.C.A. Hol, the director of a warehousing company (Blaauwhoedenveem), who until 1910 lived in the house on the street side. In 2001 the complex gained a glass roof and was recast as a trendy leisure zone. Restaurants, cafés, galleries and dance clubs now adjoin its central roofed space.

Maritime Quarter

The late nineteenth-century Maritime Quarter accommodates warehouses, the offices of port businesses and houses for the well-off. On the north side of Parklaan stand the villas of wealthy Rotterdammers, and on the south side upmarket town houses and offices. At Veerhaven there is Calandplein, an attractive public square in the shape of a quarter-circle with the Caland monument and the clubhouse of the Royal Maas Yacht Club. There are also handsome art nouveau office buildings on Veerhaven, Calandstraat and Westerkade.

37   Atlantic House

Westplein 1
P.G. Buskens
1928-1930
W.C. Brouwer (artist);
G.J. Hoorn (ren. 2003-2010)

Atlantic House is an Art Deco-style building that plays host to a miscellany of firms. Its name, detailing and artwork refer to the dynamics of harbours and ships. A major innovative feature is the internal car park. The building has a U-shaped plan and sports two round corner towers. The concrete frame dictates the rhythm of the frontage, this being a combination of brick and ponderous concrete mouldings. The building has been converted into apartments.

Hostel ROOM

In 1923 the new office building of the General Steam Navigation & Transportation Companies on the corner of Van Vollenhovenstraat and Houtlaan was opened. Hague architect J. Kooijman designed the characteristic art deco building with striking corner towers and sculpture work by Dirk Wolbers, stained glass from the Asperslag company and decorative wrought iron by Gispen. After a stint as student association and feminist club the building is now doing duty as hostel.

Gedempte Zalmhaven 47-749
W.M.J. Arets
1992-2001

Two residential tower blocks stand on a filled-in harbour basin (Gedempte Zalmhaven) near the foot of the Erasmus Bridge 🔟. Altogether the two towers boast 285 upmarket apartments. The two are joined by a plinth which includes the entrance, a parking facility and an internal street linking the lift lobbies with the towers. Communal amenities - panorama lobby, swimming pool, sauna, fitness centre, roof terrace - are on the fifth floor. The facades consist of black concrete cladding elements with a cobblestone effect created by using rubber moulds as formwork. The elongated apartment building on Zalmhaven is by DKV.

Rotterdam builds a metro

In 1968 the Rotterdam metro, the first underground railway in the Netherlands, consisted of a six kilometre line with seven stations, running from Central Station 🔲 to Zuidplein, much of it above ground. The impetus for the construction of the metro came in 1955 with the plan for a tram tunnel from Schiedamsedijk to Rijnhaven. After various extensions, the metro network now covers 78 kilometres. A trip to Spijkenisse to MVRDV's Boekenberg library (Markt 40) is well worthwhile.

Greenery

Rotterdam is often regarded as a hard city lacking in greenery, but reality confounds this perception. Indeed, in the late
1960s the Hoogvliet district was the greenest place in the
country, with forty square metres of green space per inhabitant. Rotterdam boasts several large parks: The Park **40** near the
Euromast, Plaswijck **G2**, Vroesenpark **G3**, the Kralingse Bos **G4** and
Zuiderpark **G5** in Rotterdam-Zuid.

Rotterdam's green areas have traditionally combined aes-
thetics with utility. The original motivation behind the 1954 Water
Project **8** **G6** was hygienic; but the wide-banked urban canals
(singels) were attractively designed by landscape architects. The
Kralingse Bos, laid out on the site of a fen pool in the 1930s as a
form of work creation, also accommodates the municipal plant
nursery, a riding school (W. van Tijen, 1937) and a golf course
(Brinkman & Van der Vlugt, 1933).

During the construction of the Kunsthal **35**, the former
Hoboken country estate was reconfigured as Museumpark **G7**.
Behind Museum Boijmans van Beuningen **33** lies the museum
garden with rosarium **G8**, laid out during the 1960 Floriade, and
a monument to the influential Director of Public Works G.J. de
Jongh. A new type of functional green space is the Rooftop
Park **48** **G9** along Vierhavensstraat. Below the park lies a shopping
centre complete with service road and car park.

One specific type of green space is that of cemeteries. The
Algemene Begraafplaats Crooswijk **G10** (1832), the neighbouring
Roman Catholic Cemetery **G11** (1869), the Zuiderbegraafplaats **G12**
(1940) and the Oud-Kralingen cemetery **G13** (1550) are also out-
standing parks. Another example of open-space planning combined with functionality is the zoo at Diergaarde Blijdorp **54** **G14**.

Rotterdam also has two special private gardens. Arboretum
Trompenburg **G15** started out as the country estate of the Smith
(later Van Hoey Smith) family in the nineteenth century. The
botanical garden covers eight hectares and has a unique collection of trees. The more modest Park Schoonoord **G16** is owned
by the Mees family, but is also open to the public. Near the Van
Brienenoord Bridge are two nature reserves: De Esch **G17**, along
Nesserdijk on the north bank of the Nieuwe Maas, and below the
bridge in Rotterdam-Zuid the Eiland van Brienenoord **G18**, where
you may even spot a herd of grazing Scottish Highlander cattle.

A new kind of green space is urban farming. Since the
property market crash of 2008 many unbuilt plots around the
city have been creatively transformed into modest fruit and
vegetable gardens and green playgrounds; examples include
Dakakker **G19** on top of Schieblock **5** and 'Uit je eigen Stad' **G20**
along Marconistraat **50**. The greening of the city is now part of
municipal policy. A green zone **G21** designed by landscape architect Piet Oudolf has been laid out along the banks of the Maas
near the Boompjes boulevard, the Scheepvaartkwartier and The
Park.

39 Parklaanflat

Parkstraat 2
W. van Tijen
1931-1933

Each luxury apartment in this seven-storey housing block occupies an entire floor. Van Tijen built an apartment for himself on the roof, with a spacious roof terrace looking out over the harbour. The structure consists of a steel frame with wood floors. Without knowing it Van Tijen had designed the first glass curtain wall to be built in the Netherlands. The wired glass in both external glazing and balcony partitions is painted grey where privacy requires. The building was restored in 1995. Van Tijen was the pioneer of high-rise in the Netherlands. He also designed the Bergpolderflat 56, the Plaslaanflat (Kralingse Plaslaan 120-200, 1936-1938) and the Zuidpleinflat (Zuidplein 127-393, 1940-1949).

'In 1933 there followed my first more important building: the Parklaan apartment building. It was a big gamble undertaken together with a construction company. I didn't know enough about any aspect, yet by some miracle it turned out fairly well. A decent ground plan, a steel frame, a bay window with the first glass curtain walls in the Netherlands (unbeknownst to me). Reasonable soundproofing, a roof terrace that provided contact with the Maas. I built a small house on the roof for ourselves.'

W. van Tijen, Een boekenkast opgeruimd, 1970

Westzeedijk, Parkkade
J.D. Zocher jr., L.P. Zocher
1852-1863

Known simply as The Park, this large area of green space was laid out in stages on the site of three villas. The first part was designed in 1852 by the celebrated landscape architects and garden designers Jan David Zocher jr. and his son Louis Paul Zocher. Hailing from Haarlem, the Zochers were specialists in the romantic English landscape style with its ornamental pools, rolling lawns and winding paths.
In 1875 the town council bought a fourth villa, De Heuvel, and opened its grounds to the public. When the Maas Tunnel **42** was constructed at the end of the 1930s, it meant cutting into the western edge of The Park and the sports fields located there disappeared. In 1960 the first Floriade world horticultural exhibition had a great impact on the present park's appearance. The Euromast **41** was erected and The Park, which had been seriously damaged in the 1953 floods, was cleaned up and enhanced. The Park is a regular venue for festivals and events.

Schoonoord

Famous buildings in The Park are the Orangerie, Stables and Coach House by J.F. Metzelaar, Parkzicht and the demountable Norwegian church. On Kievitslaan lies Schoonoord **G16**, a three-hundred-year-old garden belonging to a former country house, redesigned around 1860 by J.D. Zocher. In 1926 the garden came into the possession of Jacob Mees, who lived on Westzeedijk. He had the entrance, with its eighteenth-century gate, relocated to Kievitslaan. The garden has been open to the public since 1973.

Parkhaven 20
H.A. Maaskant
1958-1960
Public Works
(ext. Space Tower 1969-1970)

Designed as an attraction, this 107 metre high 'mast' consists of a concrete shaft 9 metres in diameter with a ship's bridge at 30 metres and a crow's-nest at 100 metres. The dynamically designed crow's-nest comprises an amphitheatre-shaped restaurant cantilevering a maximum of twelve metres. This steel structure was first welded, then faced and finally hoisted into position. In 1970 when the Euromast lost its record height to the Medical Faculty **34**, a slender steel shaft, the Space Tower, was added, up which a ring-shaped cabin circles to a height of 176 metres.

Rotterdam Festival City

Rotterdam's reputation as a city of festivals was born during the post-war reconstruction period when The Park hosted a number of major exhibitions. To accommodate them, large-scale complexes were constructed in The Park, including a variety of exhibition pavilions designed by well-known architects and artists. Ahoy', held in 1950 to celebrate the reconstruction of the harbour, was followed in 1955 by the National Energy Festival E55 and in 1960 by the first big international horticultural expo, Floriade. Ten years later the C70 expo was distributed across the city centre.

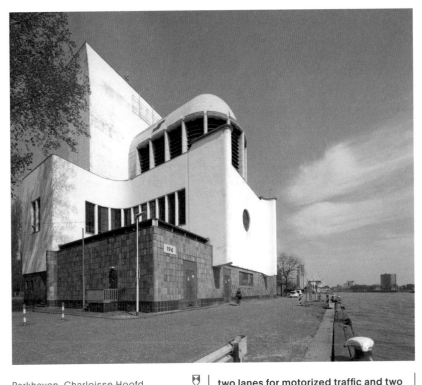

Parkhaven, Charloisse Hoofd
J.P. van Bruggen,
A. van der Steur (Public Works)
1937-1941

When the city considered building a second Maas crossing to supplement the 1878 Willems Bridge, it opted for a tunnel. The Maas Tunnel consists of two separate tubes each with two lanes for motorized traffic and two smaller tubes, one for cyclists above another for pedestrians. The concrete tunnel was prefabricated in sections which were carried by floating crane to their destination and subsequently sunk. The signature of architect Van der Steur is particularly evident in the design of the two filter houses on the north and south banks.

Pedestrian tunnel

One of Rotterdam's lesser known attractions is a walk through the Maas Tunnel. Although primarily intended for vehicles, pedestrians and cyclists can also cross to the other shore through their own dedicated tunnel tubes, which can be reached via a small entrance building and long escalators. Fans of chaste tiling work and curious phenomena like reverberation times and repeating echos will have a ball here. The mosaics are by the Rotterdam artist Jaap Gidding.

43　Müller Pier

Müllerkade, St. Jobskade
KCAP, EGM, Neutelings Riedijk,
de Architekten Cie.
1998-2007

This transformation of a dockland area into a residential district is informed by the archipelago effect on site and the great scale of the remaining harbour buildings in the vicinity. KCAP's masterplan consists of a campus-like heterogeneous system of discrete volumes and intervening public spaces. The main access to the district is a broad quay tracing its circumference. In the central zone there are some 12 housing blocks, most of them medium-rise plus three tower blocks as vertical accents. Four different architectural practices were commissioned to design these blocks, though this is scarcely noticeable as dark brick was used throughout. EGM's tower with its brick-clad facets is linked by way of the underground parking facility with Neutelings Riedijk's Humanitas old-age complex, a sculptural building with a swimming-pool as its basis.

Kröller-Müller

The Müller Pier was named after Wm.H. Müller & Co's Stuwadoors Mij. N.V., which had its premises here between 1908 and 1970. Helene Müller, daughter of the founder, married Anthony George Kröller. In 1907 she began to collect modern art by, among others, Vincent van Gogh. The Kröller-Müllers' world-famous collection was eventually housed in its own museum in the Hoge Veluwe, designed by the Belgian architect Henry Van de Velde.

Lloydstraat
J.J. Kanters; R. Winkel (Mei Architects)
1911-1914; 2000-2008
R. Winkel (Mei Architects)
(ren. 2004-2007)

At the dawn of the 21st century, a new district is taking shape close to where ships of the Rotterdam Lloyd shipping company used to lie at anchor. The old brick office building of Rotterdam Lloyd has been partially recast as residential units. Built in phases, the Schiecentrale project comprises business premises for the audiovisual and creative sector, cafés and restaurants, and housing. The original Schiecentrale building, dating from 1905, was fitted out with recording studios. The 25kV building contains office spaces, while the power station became Hotel Stroom. The Kraton Building, whose tenants include RTV Rijnmond, is clad with cast iron facade panels. Completing the Schiecentrale complex are two high-rise blocks containing apartments and offices. The Jobsveem warehouse is 130 metres long, 25 metres wide and 25 metres high with a total floor area of 19,000 m², with concrete foundations and concrete loading balconies facing the quayside. The robust building, which lost its warehousing role in the late 1980s, has been converted into apartments. Three atria with glass-roofed stairwells admit daylight deep into the building. The apartments line two sides of a corridor; the ground floor is reserved for commercial space.

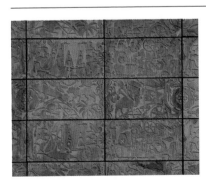

Cast iron

The elevations of the Kraton Building in the Schiecentrale complex are clad with cast iron facade panels, a seemingly less obvious choice of material, but it has its advantages. After a few years of rusting it becomes maintenance-free and the rugged, dark brown appearance is perfect in the context of the docks and large-scale buildings. The reliefs in eight different patterns, designed by Studio Job, depict the history and future of the port.

45   Shipping and Transport College

Lloydstraat 300
Neutelings Riedijk
2000-2005

The premises of the Shipping and Transport College have gathered together in one prominent place a number of institutes of learning formerly scattered across the city. The 2000 or so students receiving secondary and higher vocational education here have a magnificent view out over their future field of operation. The cantilevered apex of the blue and white checked building, which has everything of a periscope, contains the lecture hall. The broad low-rise portion is given over to practical classrooms, simulation spaces, sports halls and a large canteen. Vertical circulation among the 16 storeys is by way of escalators set centrally in the building. The facade is assembled from elements measuring 3.6 x 3.8 metres: white and blue aluminium panels, glass and perforated profiled sheets. Inside, sturdy materials such as timber, steel and canvas prevail along with sundry associations with the shipping world. For example, the acoustics in the lecture hall are regulated by cladding the walls with red air cushions. The rooms have portholes and wall units that refer to ship's timbers. Ship's benches assembled from wooden slats stand here and there.

Beside the Maas I often stand lost in thought.
Beside the Maas I've dreamt many a dream.
I love docks and cranes,
Silos and grain.
And I love a ship on the open water.

Hans Ruf jr., song

Mathenesserdijk 410-422
R. Winkel (Mei Architects)
2011-2012
Architect unknown
(orig. des. 1896-1926)

Roeloff's uitstoomingsinrichting, stoomververij en chemische wasserij NV established its steam laundry business in a few old buildings in Delfshaven in 1892. In 1926 the complex was extended with a functionalist factory section along the Schie waterway. The building, which had deteriorated into a ruin after being squatted by artists in the late 1980s, was transformed in 2011 into a multi-tenanted building for creative entrepreneurs. In the central zone, where the traditional houses and the industrial complex converge, is an atrium with staircases, lift, meeting places and the entrance to the 36 units. A glass roof, lightwells and glass internal walls ensure that daylight penetrates deep into the building. It is here, too, that the leap in scale between the various storey heights is resolved. The complex encompasses a restaurant and a roof terrace for the tenants.

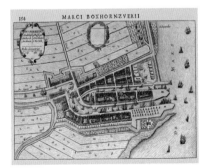

Rotterdam is many villages

In 1389 Delft acquired an outpost on the Nieuwe Maas river: Delfshaven. It became independent of Delft in 1817 and remained so until being annexed by Rotterdam in 1886. The old core of Delfshaven is still largely intact. Elsewhere in the city it is possible to distinguish the old cores of other annexed villages: Overschie, Schiebroek, Hillegersberg, Terbregge, Kralingen, Charlois and IJsselmonde. Some of these villages have a history stretching back further than that of Rotterdam. Pernis, Hoogvliet, Hoek van Holland and Rozenburg now belong to the municipality of Rotterdam as well.

47   Le Medi

Oaseplein & environs
Geurst & Schulze
2002-2008
Korteknie Stuhlmacher (assoc.);
A. Coenen (artist)

Le Medi is an urban block of 103 hous-ing units in the 'problem neighbour-hood' of Delfshaven. The original concept was developed by multicul-tural entrepreneur Hassani Idrissi and One Architecture. From the outside, the block registers as a solid city wall with sturdily detailed window open-ings. Quasi-Moorish 'city gates' give access to a Mediterranean central court, a separate world of short streets, colourful fronts and informal texture. The little streets lead into a formal courtyard inspired by the architec-ture of Southern Europe; the straight line of the water feature is a reference to the Alhambra. More generally, the ornamentation of plinths, brickwork, fencing and the like contain African, Andalusian and Arabic motifs.

Forgotten bombardment

When the Allies undertook a bombing raid over Rotterdam on 31 March 1943, they mistakenly hit the area at the end of Schiedamseweg instead of their intended target, the German Kriegsmarine complex at Vierhaven. More than 2600 houses were destroyed. This reconstruction project (the 'forgotten bom-bardment') consists of housing with shops on Schiedamseweg and five east-west oriented eight-storey blocks of gallery-access flats with elegant concrete entrances zones. In 1993 a memor-ial by Matthieu Ficheroux was installed in the park on the Gijsinglaan.

Vierhavensstraat
Buro Sant en Co; Butzelaar Van Son
2009-2011

A disused railyard in the western docklands was replaced with an unusual
example of dual land use: a park for
the local Bospolder community on top
of the roof of a commercial strip. The
latter is 650 metres long and intended
for relatively large stores of between
800 and 5000 m², such as supermar-
kets and furniture stores. On the street
side the stores have a double-height
glass facade in a brick surround; they
are supplied via a delivery lane at
the rear. On the first floor, above and
behind the shops, is a car park with
750 spaces. A massive concrete structure supports the rooftop park with
lawns, water features, trees and a play-
ground. Beside the greenhouse-style
café pavilion is stair linking the park
with the shops.

*'This is a city for people who don't want to
be bothered. Rotterdam is a bit disjointed
and that has its attractions. In other cities
everything has its place. If you don't go to the
right parties you soon become an outsider. The
nice thing about Rotterdam is that you don't feel
obliged to take part in those kinds of scenes.'*

Adriaan Geuze, Rotterdam herzien, 2007

49   Haka Building

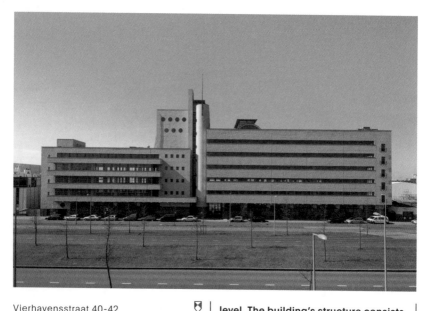

Vierhavensstraat 40-42
H.F. Mertens, J. Koeman
1931-1932

Built for a cooperative wholesalers'
society (De Handelskamer), the Haka
Building comprises offices and commercial space, storage zones, a silo
and a factory. Owing to the narrow-
ness of the available site (15 metres),
wedged as it is between quay wall and
roadway, all storeys except the ground
floor cantilever 2.3 metres on both
sides. Rails below the jutting first floor
enable wagons to load at ground floor
level. The building's structure consists
of a concrete frame with lightweight
partition walls. The cooperative was
dissolved in the 1960s; the building
was restored in 2010.

M4H

Merwe-Vierhavens (M4H) is a docks area
that is gradually being transformed into a
centre for the creative industry. Industrial
buildings like the Cotton Warehouse, the
Glazed Building, the Gateway Building
of Thomsen's Havenbedrijf and the Fruit
Auction Complex provide spaces for artists and designers like Joep van Lieshout,
Richard Hutten and Daan Roosegaarde,
as well as for the Food Bank. The gas-
ometer has been reincarnated as the
Ferro Dome, the Keilewerf is a centre
for making all manner of things and the
Design Dock, Marconistraat 52 and the
Diepeveenbuilding are multi-occupancy
buildings for architects and designers.

50 Europoint

Galvanistraat 15
G.J. Jarik, M. Goldschmidt,
W.E. Dunlap (SOM)
1971-1975

What began in 1968 as an overblown design for a World Trade Centre in two towers at Leuvehaven in the city centre was eventually realized in a slightly modified form as the Europoint three-tower complex on Marconiplein. The elevations of white travertine cladding and tinted glass in bronze-coloured frames look rational and abstract yet have been given every aesthetic consideration. Each successive storey widens by just a few centimetres as a perspective-correcting device. The two towers linked by a low entry block used to house the Urban Planning and Public Housing Agency, which relocated to De Rotterdam **78** in 2013. The third tower is currently occupied by an educational institution.

Locally grown

The enthusiasm with which residents have recently taken to growing produce on every little patch of empty ground in the city has also prompted a number of larger initiatives. The best-known of these is 'Uit je eigen Stad' **G20**, an urban farm on Marconistraat. The aim is to reconnect city dwellers with the food that ends up on their plate every day. Food is grown there and, along with regional produce, sold in a market and in a restaurant. There are also regular workshops, tastings, tours, events and children's activities.

51   Justus van Effen Complex

Justus van Effenstraat & environs
M. Brinkman
1919-1922
Molenaar & Co., Hebly Theunissen
(rest. 2000-2012)

In 1919 Michiel Brinkman designed a complex of 273 dwellings in the Spangen district. Commissioned by the Municipal Housing Authority, it exploits the possibilities of the perimeter block to the full. One large block of 147 by 85 metres enfolds a courtyard containing a few smaller blocks and a central taller building comprising the central heating plant, baths and cycle shelter. A public street running through the large block forks at the facilities building. A new feature for those days was the use of an access gallery, a raised walkway along the block's inner edge. This permitted a high housing density without having to resort to complicated space-consuming stair towers. Almost all dwellings are entered from the inner courtyard. Units on the ground and first floors are accessed at ground level and have their own garden. Above these are two maisonettes reached from the access gallery. All units have central heating (a first for Dutch social housing) and a rubbish chute. The courtyard is entered through four striking gateways, one on each side. Ten staircases and two goods lifts for tradesmen's handcarts lead to the access gallery which, with its ample width of 2.2-3.3 metres, functions as a raised street, a children's play area and a balcony for neighbourly contact and door-to-door services. Plant boxes, tiled artwork and peep-holes for children enliven this concrete gallery. Initial criticism of the plan was crushed thanks to the intervention of Auguste Plate, director of the Municipal Housing Authority, and various socialist aldermen. This criticism was levelled especially at its 'un-Dutch' character, the emphasis on collectivity and its costly amenities. There were fears, too, that the combination of flat roofs and access galleries would lead to 'dangers of a moral nature'. In 2012 the complex was completely restored and all traces of previous renovations erased. A large variety of housing types was realized, the courtyard was redesigned and the facilities building given a new use.

'That two-metre space would become an endless
to-do of children playing, neighbours arguing and
suppliers fighting. What's more, the 264 families will
share one big flat roof and Mr Verheul was very much
afraid that it would be used for orgies that would
raise a blush in the Hanging Gardens of Babylon.'

Rotterdamsch Nieuwsblad, 17 April 1920

52 Van Nelle Factory

Van Nelleweg 1
Brinkman & Van der Vlugt
1925-1931
J.G. Wiebenga (struc. eng.),
M.A. Stam (assoc.);
Claessens Erdmann,
W. de Jonge (rest. 1999-2003)
(Visit via UrbanGuides)

Van der Vlugt became involved in the construction of this coffee, tea and tobacco factory after the death of Michiel Brinkman. The factory's design is in many ways revolutionary. Besides optimum functioning of the factory, great emphasis was placed on providing improved working conditions for the employees.

The factory proper occupies three volumes of decreasing height, one of eight levels for tobacco, a coffee section of five levels with a double-height entresol, and a three-level tea department. These three factory zones are interlinked by volumes containing stairs, toilets, washrooms and space for lifts. Each stair tower has its own form of stair. At the rear of the tobacco section is a warehouse with a sawtooth roof. All three zones adjoin a main service route and are further connected by bridges (almost the hallmark of this factory) to a row along the water of dispatch and storage spaces, a cycle shelter, a boiler house and workshops. The entrance to the grounds is marked by a freestanding office building whose facade follows the curve of the service route. The circular tea room on the roof of the tobacco factory section was added during construction to allow continued enjoyment of the view.

The factory's concrete floor slabs are supported by concrete mushroom columns, leaving facades column-free, a condition borne out by continuous strips of fenestration which flood the work areas with daylight.

Since Van Nelle's departure in 1995, the building has been restored and begun a new life as Van Nelle Design Factory. The restoration endeavoured to maintain the transparency of the factory floors by installing the new facades required for climate control on the inside. On the upper floors business premises of varying sizes were carved out for the creative sector. The ground floor is suitable for exhibitions and conferences. The ancillary buildings have also been restored and are now occupied by architecture firms. In 2014 the Van Nelle Factory was added to UNESCO's World Heritage List.

'Voici le poème de la lumière. Le lyrisme de l'impeccable. L'éclat de l'ordre. L'atmosphère de la droiture. ...Je dis que la visite de cette usine fut l'un des beaux jours de ma vie.'

Le Corbusier, 1932

53 De Schie Penitentiary

Professor Jonkersweg 7/Abraham van Stolkweg
C.J.M. Weeber (de Architekten Cie.)
1985-1989

Carel Weeber's flirtation with Classicism and the Rationalist Jean-Nicolas Durand has resulted here in a fully blank-walled block with facades in vivid hues, surrounded by a rusticated prison wall five metres high. The rectangular penitentiary of 80 x 200 metres enfolds two courtyards. Two hundred and fifty-two cells flank the long sides of the courtyards and the recreation rooms the short sides; all spaces look onto the yards. In the interior too, the bright colours and artworks poke fun at the grim nature of the brief.

Classic escape

Eleven months after the opening on 24 October 1990, three prisoners attempted to escape from De Schie through a tunnel to the courtyard; one of them was then able to climb over the outer wall using a rope. In the Volkskrant, the architect Carel Weeber expressed his admiration for this 'splendid, classic' escape: 'We had ruled it out as impossible because the groundwater is pretty high.'

54 Blijdorp Zoo ☕ 🍴

Van Aerssenlaan 49, Blijdorplaan 8
S. van Ravesteyn
1937-1941
L. Bolle, W. van Kuilenburg,
J.W. Uiterwaal (artists)

A few Van Ravesteyn buildings, including the old entrance, the giraffe
enclosure and part of the Rivièrahal,
have been restored.

Indoor and outdoor accommodations
of animals are grouped along the principal axis following the length of the
park. The main block, the Rivièrahal,
adjoins the houses for primates,
pachyderms and tropical fauna. Each
building's decoration sets out to symbolize its occupants' place of origin.
The curve, a recurring formal theme in
Van Ravesteyn's work, is to be found
here in abundance. Between 1990 and
2001 an eleven-hectare site containing
the Oceanium and a new entrance was
added to the zoo. Many of the buildings have been altered or replaced
over the years at the cost of the overall concept, not least due to the additional entrance in the new extension.

There are zebras walking down Coolsestraat

The old zoo (Diergaarde) was in the centre of Rotterdam, on
the appropriately named Diergaardesingel. The bombardment
of May 1940 took place after some animals had already been
relocated to the new premises in Blijdorp. Tales of lions and
tigers roaming the burning streets are urban myths; they had
already been shot by soldiers. Several small monkeys had indeed
escaped and were spotted here and there around the city.

55 De Eendracht

Vroesenlaan/Van der Horststraat/
Navanderstraat
J.H. van den Broek
1929-1935

Dating from the 1930s, De Eendracht
occupies an important place in Dutch
architectural history in the transi-
tion from perimeter block to open
planning. The other blocks along
Vroesenlaan are of the traditional
perimeter type. De Eendracht is open
on the park side and enfolds a large
ornamental garden. One of its corners contains a children's playroom.
The dwellings are raised half a storey
above street level allowing for storage, wash and play space below and
are concrete-framed, a rarity in those
days. Sliding glass partitions permit
a change of internal subdivision
between day and night.

56 Bergpolderflat

Dr. de Visserstraat 65-207
W. van Tijen, Brinkman & Van der Vlugt
1932-1934
Op ten Noort Blijdenstein
(rest. 1992-1993)

The Bergpolderflat constitutes the prototype for many later slab-shaped housing blocks. Several Rotterdam contractors plucked up courage and tackled the experiment of high-rise workers' housing themselves. The motivation for building high in Rotterdam was not aesthetic, but of an economic, social and practical nature. The high-rise blocks were based on the advantages to health of sun and air, the possibilities of ample green space in-between blocks and the economic advantages of a thorough-going standardization and prefabrication, leading to competitive rents.
The building consists of nine levels of housing each containing eight identical gallery-access flats. Access galleries are reached using a lift located behind the glazed stair tower at the building's head. The dwellings were only six metres wide by eight metres deep, but sliding doors and glass walls made them feel quite spacious. The building's structure consists of a steel frame with X-shaped wind braces between the lightweight sandstone partition walls. Floors alternate upwards between two of wood and one of concrete as a fire precaution. Stairs, access galleries and balcony floors are of prefabricated concrete. The timber fronts with movable steel components are prefabricated too. On the ground floor are storage spaces and washing and drying facilities which are still used today. A low-lying volume set square to the slab relates this ostensibly alien high-rise element to the street pattern of its surroundings, marks the entrance and screens the communal gardens from the street. These extra amenities are the main reason why living in this high rise has a quality almost entirely lacking in its successors of later years. The building has been restored and the small dwelling units adapted to satisfy current standards.

Gallery flat

The Bergpolderflat's galleries were an innovative form of access. In many respects the Bergpolderflat is the prototype for a whole series of post-war apartment buildings. These so-called 'gallery flats' were built all over the Netherlands, including in the centre of Rotterdam on the Lijnbaan 12. The quality of the first exemplars was never replicated, however, and the gallery flat became synonymous with shoddy, cheap housing. 'Like a numbered inmate of Sing Sing, the Rotterdam worker trudges along the gallery of his flat building, searching for the number of his "home",' wrote M.J. Granpré Molière in the Rooms Katholiek Bouwblad of 1935.

Noordsingel 113-117
W.C. Metzelaar
1895-1899
A.C. Pierson (Huis van Bewaring
1863-1872)

Formerly housing the district courts, this building was designed by W.C. Metzelaar who was appointed architectural engineer for prisons and courthouses in 1883. Built in neo-Renaissance style, its symmetrical facade sports decorative yellow brickwork with freestone dressings. Behind it lies an earlier work, A.C. Pierson's prison complex of 1872, reached through a gateway in the courthouse with statues of Justitia, a sage and a supplicant atop its pediment. In 1996 the law courts moved to new premises at Kop van Zuid **72**; the prison was closed in 2012. The complex will be converted into housing and renamed De Tuin van Noord.

Panopticum

In 1863 the Netherlands' first cellular prison was built here, a so-called wing prison in the form of a star with four cell wings and one administration wing. From the central hub guards could survey all 340 cells. Prison, exercise yard and church – the first 'prison church' to be built in the Netherlands – were all rigidly cellular: the prisoners were unable to see one another. There were even cellular vans for transporting prisoners.

58 Technikon

Schiekade/Benthemstraat
Maaskant, Van Dommelen, Kroos, Senf
1955-1970
C.K. Appel (artist)

This huge complex housing eight technical schools consists of three freestanding building parts atop and linked by a continuous basement. The main portion, ten storeys high, 220 metres long and 22.5 metres deep, follows the curve of the former Hofplein rail viaduct **61**. The shared great hall halfway along the main block doubles as a theatre and sports an expressive sculpture in concrete and stained glass by Karel Appel. The intermediate building square to the main block serves to link the latter to an 11-storey tower boasting eight gymnasiums and a swimming pool.

Water Square

Designed by De Urbanisten the courtyard of the school complex has been turned into a 'Water Square': in an interesting combination of civil engineering and landscape architecture a number of basins disguised as skate ramp, dance floor, playing field and spectator stand have been constructed for the temporary collection of rainwater. The aim is to relieve pressure on street drains during periods of heavy rainfall and is part of the city's strategy to climate-proof Rotterdam.

59 Hofdijk

Stroveer & environs
J. Verhoeven
1977-1983

This project was an attempt to design a housing estate 'with an individual identity yet part and parcel of Rotterdam'. This was done by having the River Rotte thread through the plan; by assembling a unified estate from small manageable elements though with the repetition of stylized 'Rotterdam roofs' to identify individual units; by using streets-in-the-air to provide units with a maximum of 'street' access; and by creating an atmosphere in which 'the fullest possible reflection of life may be expressed'. The project, typical of the 1970s cult of the small-scale, is known locally as Gnomesville or Little Volendam.

60 Ammersooiseplein

Ammersooiseplein 1-33
DKV
1984-1988

Instead of the required perimeter block, the architects proposed a transparent open row layout combining a tall housing slab with a less-tall block of business premises with dwellings above. This stacking created space for a public square. The dwellings on the two lowest levels of the housing slab are oriented to the square; those on the upper floors, reached from access galleries, to the city. This homage to modernism proves that the slab-shaped apartment block, if designed with care, is still a practicable building type.

Gnomesville

In the 1970s there was an attempt to generate greater liveliness and atmosphere in the impersonal reconstructed centre by building cheery, small-scale houses, constructing terraces and pavilions, introducing more greenery and calling a halt to office construction. The small-scale housing on Hofdijk, Sint-Jacobsplaats, around Oudehaven 26 and on the Leuvehaven jetties is typical of this period.

Raampoortstraat, Vijverhofstraat
A.C.C.G. van Hemert (HBG)
1899-1908
PEÑA Architecture (ren. Mini Mall
2008-2011)

This concrete viaduct was constructed at the turn of the century by the then new Zuid-Holland electric railway company (ZHESM) for a rail link between Hofplein and Scheveningen. It is one of the first large concrete structures in the Netherlands. The enterprise specially set up to construct it would later become the HBG construction company. The viaduct consists of 189 arches, whose openings were colonized by warehouses, shops and companies. The arrival of Randstadrail has made the Hofplein Viaduct redundant. The first section of the Hofbogen has been restored and now houses trendy cafés and shops. The green roof connects with the new 'air bridge' 5 and can be used for events. The rest of the almost two kilometre long heritage structure will eventually be restored and made publicly accessible.

Vrouwe Groenevelt's Liefdegesticht

Founded in 1814 and designed by B. Hooijkaas jr., this charity-run housing originally began life at another address. In fact it has had to move twice, first in 1864 from Oostsingel when a new street was laid out and then in 1900 from Weenaplein for safety reasons when the Hofplein Viaduct was built. Since 1902 the 16 almshouses have stood at Vijverhofstraat. The tile picture on the facade above the trustees' room is a survivor from the first address. It shows a pair of demonic figures being driven away by two angels leaning on a clock.

Art in public space

Rotterdam has an extensive collection of modern art in public space. During the reconstruction period people were actively encouraged to enliven facades by means of murals, mosaics and reliefs, and several commissions were awarded for modern sculptures on important sites in the city. Initially the notion of infusing the empty city centre with meaning would have been an important motivation, but gradually the idea of building up a collection of art in public space developed. Nowadays the city is an open-air museum for modern sculpture.

A1   Ossip Zadkine,
The Destroyed City, Plein 40-45, 1951

A2   Henry Moore,
Wall Relief No. 1, Weena, 1954

A3   Fred Carasso,
The Bow, Boompjes, 1956

A4   Naum Gabo,
Untitled ('The Thing'), De Bijenkorf, Coolsingel, 1957

A5   Auguste Rodin,
L'Homme Qui Marche, Westersingel sculpture terrace, 1961 (1905)

A6   Giacomo Manzú,
War and Peace, doors of St. Laurenskerk, 1968

A7   George Rickey,
Two Turning Vertical Rectangles, Binnenwegplein, 1969

A8   Pablo Picasso, Carl Nesjar,
Sylvette, Westersingel, 1970

A9   Willem de Kooning,
Seated Woman, Reclining Figure, Standing Figure, Weena, 1970, 1969, 1969

A10   Claes Oldenburg,
Screw Arch, Museumtuin, 1982

A11   Auke de Vries,
Maas Sculpture, Willems Bridge, 1982

A12   Coop Himmelb(l)au,
The Long, Thin, Yellow Legs of Architecture, Vasteland, 1988

A13   John Körmeling,
1989, Hillekopplein, 1991

A14   Lebbeus Woods,
The Hermitage, Het Nieuwe Instituut, Museumpark, 1999

A15   Franz West,
Qwertz, Eendrachtsweg, 2000

A16   Jeff Wall,
Lost Luggage Depot, Koninginnehoofd, 2001

A17   Paul McCarthy,
Santa Claus, Eendrachtsplein, 2001

A18   Giuseppe Penone,
Elevazione, Westersingel, 2001

A19   Atelier Van Lieshout,
Cascade, Churchillplein, 2009

A20   Arno Coenen, Iris Roskam, *Horn of Plenty*, Markthal, Binnenrotte, 2014

A1

A2

A3

A4

A5

A6

A7

A8

A9

A10

A11

A12

A13

A14

A15

A16

A17

A18

A19

A20

62   Houben House

Built for two of the architects of Mecanoo, this house is configured much like the house of Van Nelle director Kees van der Leeuw at no. 38: a design studio on the ground floor, the living room on the first floor with a generous view of the lake (Kralingse Plas) and bedrooms and library on the second floor. Its architecture draws on the more elegant modernism of the past (Eames, Aalto) and has a many-layered, open spatial composition. It runs the gamut of materials most of which are left in their untreated 'natural' state.

Kralingse Plaslaan 88
F.M.J. Houben, E.L.J.M. van Egeraat
(Mecanoo)
1989-1991

63   Van den Broek House

Van den Broek's own house consists of a large, rectangular block containing the garage, bedroom, workroom and double-height living room with mezzanine floor, and a smaller block of entrance and kitchen. It is all but closed to the street; the garden elevation by contrast can be fully opened up using glazed sliding partitions two storeys high. This side also has a balcony with steel stair. The white-rendered brick walls are loadbearing. Round steel columns stand along the garden elevation. 'It is the only postwar house in which I have felt anything more than despair, here architecture lives,' the English architect Peter Smithson observed in 1954.

Kralingseweg 179
J.H. van den Broek
1948-1952

Stamping Ground

The Netherlands boasts its very own Woodstock. In the summer of 1970 the Kralingse Bos ᴳ⁴ was the site of the Holland Pop Festival, a three-day event featuring the likes of Jefferson Airplane, Santana, The Byrds, Soft Machine and many more. Pink Floyd closed the festival. Like Woodstock, the festival was legendary not so much because of the quality of the music, but because of the free love and soft drugs on offer, overseen by a handful of police and volunteers. In 2013 a monument to the festival was unveiled on Plaszoom.

64 Two Patio Villas

Onderlangs 44-46
OMA
1985-1989

Here, two linked villas are set against the bank of a road so that the street side has two storeys and the garden side only one. The ground floor contains the entrance, a garage, a guest room and a fitness room toplit from the patio. The living space round the patio (which may be opened up) recalls the villa and apartment plans, so admired by Koolhaas, of Mies van der Rohe. The materiality and detailing, such as the floating roof, sloping walls and colour planes that deny the functional division into two, are allusions to the 1950s.

Rubbish dump

Shortly after the war, the former Kralingen rubbish dump was transformed into an upmarket residential area. The best-known house was the experimental, virtually wholly glazed home of Herman Haan (Kralingseweg 187), which was later radically remodelled. Joost Boks also had his own house there (Bovenover 12). In the 1980s another row of villas was built on the embankment beside the Ringvaart. Herman de Kovel's own house (Kralingseweg 195) is the latest addition.

Clazina Kouwenbergzoom/Jacques
Dutilhweg
Mecanoo
1989-1993

The Prinsenland expansion area in the east of Rotterdam lies not on the city outskirts, but is wedged between the large-scale high-rise district of Alexanderpolder and pre-war Kralingen. The original characteristics, open ribbon development with mature gardens and a fine mesh of drainage ditches and meadows, have been preserved wherever possible. The Ringvaartplas District is a latter-day garden suburb, dominated by yellow and terracotta colours. The heart is made up of eight rows of three gently rotated blocks of housing set on a residential path. The rows are separated alternately by a road or a theme garden. All dwellings face south and are accessed by a footpath running between the north side and the ends of the gardens of the succeeding block. The area is closed off along the edges by taller development. Its east side is terminated by an elongated apartment building that steps up to six storeys, a pair of crescents and one more block of path-accessed dwellings.

Lowest point in the Netherlands

Several municipalities lay claim to being the lowest point in the Netherlands. The Alexander Polder's seven metres below the mean sea level (NAP) was celebrated in an artwork in Prinsenpark by Frans de Wit in 1996. Het Vierkant Eiland in de Plas (The Square Island in the Lake) consists of a 52 by 52 metre concrete slab accessible via two narrow walkways, topped by a canted, 30 metre diameter concrete dish. In the middle of the dish is a 3 by 3 metre hole containing water.

Erasmus University's main campus is a long way from the city centre in the suburb of Kralingen. Three building parts - a utilitarian high-rise slab of faculties and institutes, a sculptural wing of lecture halls and a general assembly hall cum senate wing - assemble round a square terminated by an aerial walkway. A library building standing in the water extends the line of the lecture hall wing. The expressive concrete architecture and 'bourgeois' cladding were fairly unenthusiastically received on delivery, at a time when the wave of democratization was at its peak. In the 1980s the complex was extended with new buildings for administration and lecture halls designed by Wim Quist. In 2007 work began on a new campus with more green space, fewer parking lots, cycle and pedestrian paths and liveliness in the form of student housing and the Erasmus Pavilion, a square glass box containing a vaulted auditorium clad with wooden slats.

Burgemeester Oudlaan 50
Elffers Van der Heyden Hoogeveen
1963-1970
D.C. Elffers, C. K. Appel, H. Petri (artists);
W.G. Quist (ext. 1987-1991, 1990-1994);
De Zwarte Hond, Powerhouse Company
(Erasmus Pavilion 2010-2013)

School of Commerce

In 2013 Erasmus University celebrated its centenary, although strictly speaking Rotterdam did not acquire a university until 1973 when the Medical Faculty merged with the Netherlands School of Economics. The latter was in turn the continuation of the Netherlands School of Commerce, which was founded in 1913 and largely funded by the Rotterdam business community. Between 1916 and 1968 the school occupied a striking building on Pieter de Hoochweg 222 (today's Theatre School).

Watertorenweg & environs
C.B. van der Tak; A. van der Steur
(Public Works)
1871-1873; 1928-1929
Renovation and new-build 1983-1996

The Rotterdam waterworks (DWL) were established in 1873 on Oude Plantage at the north end of Honingerdijk, far beyond the town limits of those days. Before then, Rotterdam's residents drew their drinking water from the filthy canals and moats with regular outbreaks of cholera as a result. In the new complex, designed by the Town Architect C.B. van der Tak, river water was purified in two large settling tanks and four smaller filter tanks. A 48 metre tall round water tower with a reservoir of 1000 m3 at the top, displays in its architecture a mix of Romanesque,

Neo-Renaissance and Moorish styles. When the DWL moved out in 1977 the site was transformed into a residential area. Many of the existing buildings were retained and recycled, such as the water tower, which was appropriated in 1978 by the Utopia live-work community. This was the first step in the metamorphosis from industrial complex to residential area, whose layout is predicated on the pattern of the original filter tanks. The former pumping station has been refurbished as a community and shopping centre; the original filter houses have been recast as residential units for one to two persons.

Utopia

Creative incubators are firmly entrenched in the contemporary city. One of the oldest in Rotterdam is the live-work community Utopia, which started in 1977 when a group of architecture students and artists took over a deserted waterworks. Hal 4 hosted performances by the Cure, New Order and Captain Beefheart. 010 Publishers, the leading publisher in the field of architecture, had its beginnings here.

68 Waterworks

Schaardijk 150
W.G. Quist
1973-1977

Wim Quist designed a trio of complexes for the Rotterdam water company. This complex on Schaardijk
consists of a storage basin, a pumping
station, a dosing block, a filter plant,
a staff building and two large drop-
let-shaped clear-water reservoirs. The
staff building has splayed corners
relating it to factories on the other side
of the motorway. Laboratories, workshops and offices stand along its central corridor. The whole constitutes a
perfect example of engineer's architecture in its varied construction and
attention to detail.

Berenplaat

Wim Quist was the Rotterdam water company's regular designer. Apart from the
complex on Schaardijk, he also designed
Petrusplaat in De Biesbosch (1974) and
Berenplaat (1965). That last and oldest
complex in particular is a futuristic-look-
ing feat of civil engineering, in which
every building was designed specifically
for the function it fulfilled in the water
purification process.

69   Willems Bridge

In the 1970s the old steel Willems Bridge linking Noordereiland and the north bank of the Maas was replaced by a new bridge able to accommodate the increase in traffic. Its deck is held aloft by a system of tie rods attached to two V-shaped steel towers the colour of red lead. Almost immediately on completion the new Willems Bridge joined the skyline of the new high-rises along Boompjes boulevard as one of the most engaging icons of what was once again a dynamic city.

Willemsbrug
C. Veerling (Public Works)
1975-1981
A. de Vries (artist)

70   Erasmus Bridge

Erasmusbrug
Van Berkel & Bos
1990-1996

Following the success of the Willems Bridge 69 and convinced of the monumental symbolism a bridge can emanate, the City of Rotterdam decided that the new suspension bridge should symbolize Rotterdam in the year 2000. From the very first sketches, the 'Swan', as this expressively angled pylon level with Noordereiland was immediately dubbed, has caught the public imagination. The bridge's design has been thought through down to the smallest details. Van Berkel & Bos also designed the approaches and a pleasure-boat booking office with single-level car park on the north bank. The quay at the south side and the bridgehouse were designed by Bolles + Wilson.

Roundabout

For twenty years the site of a new bridge or tunnel to replace the old Willems Bridge of 1879 was the subject of designs and, more especially, debate. The idea was to link Mariniersweg directly with Oranjeboomstraat by means of a giant roundabout, 300 metres in diameter, at Oudehaven. A sort of motorway interchange in the middle of the city. The new Willems Bridge did eventually get built, but in order to spare the historical Oudehaven, the traffic route meanders rather illogically through the city via the so-called Lus van Linthorst.

Koningshaven
P. Joosting
1924-1927

The railway lifting-bridge, known as 'De Hef', shared with the characteristic Koninginnebrug and the old Willems Bridge **69** the task of linking the central island (Noordereiland) with the banks of the River Maas. Without doubt the most eulogized bridge in the Netherlands, it has a special place in the hearts of Rotterdammers and is a perpetual source of inspiration for poets, film-makers and architects. Made redundant when the railway tunnel was built below the Maas in 1993, the Hef was saved from impending demolition by the ensuing storm of protest. In 2000 it was even declared a national monument; restoration work is scheduled to begin in autumn 2015. On 14 January 1933 the Rotterdammer Lou Vlasblom executed a somersault dive from the 67 metre high Hef into the waters of the Koningshaven. A week later an out-of-work seaman who tried to do the same did not survive the jump.

'The Hef is full of movement, something I crave. Look here: Amsterdam–Paris trains fly over it, powerfully propelled by black metal and white steam. Here, too, are big, slow ships arriving from the high seas, or leaving the city. The Hef itself creates, with its big vertical movements, a diversity of activity: revolving vanes, quivering cables.'

Cornelis Bastiaan Vaandrager, De Hef, 1975

High-rise

When it was built in 1898, the eleven-storey, 45 metre high Witte Huis 🄴 was the tallest office building in Europe. Yet it was to take almost a century for Rotterdam to develop into the high-rise capital of the Netherlands. The municipal council actually banned high-rise in the 1970s (when the tower on Hofplein was completed in 1976, alderman Hans Mentink called it 'the final erection of big business'), but in the decades that followed attitudes underwent a dramatic change. Rotterdam acquired metropolitan ambitions and pursued an active policy of central city consolidation, spawning a wave of high-rise projects. Initially this taller development was centred on Weena 🄴 and along the banks of the Maas 🄴, but it is on Kop van Zuid 🄴 that the city is gradually realizing its 'Manhattan on the Maas' ambitions.

The tallest buildings in Rotterdam

Het Witte Huis 🄴, Wijnhaven 3, W. Molenbroek, 1897-1898   45 m.
GEB-gebouw, Rochussenstraat 230-736, W.G. Witteveen, J. Poot, A.   64 m.
van der Steur, 1927-1930
Euromast 🄴, Parkhaven 20, H.A. Maaskant, 1958-1960   104 m.
PTT communications tower, Anthony Fokkerweg, Kraaijvanger   106 m.
Architecten, 1961-1965
Medical Faculty 🄴, Dr. Molewaterplein 40, OD 205, 1965-1968   114 m.
Spacetower Euromast 🄴, Parkhaven 20, H.A. Maaskant, 1970   185 m.
Delftse Poort 🄴, Weena 505, A. Bonnema, 1986-1991   151 m.
Montevideo 🄴, Landverhuizersplein 1-152, F.M.J. Houben   151 m.
(Mecanoo), 1999-2005
Maastoren, Wilhelminakade 1, Dam & Partners, 2005-2010   164 m.
PTT communications tower, Anthony Fokkerweg, 1989   207 m.
Shell Pernis refinery stack, Vondelingenweg 601, 1968   213 m.

The tallest residential buildings in Rotterdam

Parklaanflat 🄴, Parkstraat 2, W. van Tijen, 1931-1933   30 m.
Apartment building, Ungerplein, J.H. van den Broek, 1931-1936   43 m.
Maastorenflat, Schiedamsedijk 155-200, H.D. Bakker, 1955-1956   45 m.
Zusterflat Hoge Wiek, Oostmolenwerf 30, Kraaijvanger Architecten,   53 m.
1967
Six tower blocks Ommoord, Arrheniusweg, J. Nust, 1972   62 m.
Hoge Wiek apartment building, Prinsenlaan 101-571, J.P. Landers,   69 m.
1974
Three apartment buildings, Boompjes 266-666, Klunder   69 m.
Architecten, 1980-1989.
Weena Tower, Weena 181-323, Klunder Architecten, 1982-1990   106 m.
Montevideo 🄴, Landverhuizersplein 1-152, F.M.J. Houben   151 m.
(Mecanoo), 1999-2005
New Orleans 🄴, Van der Hoevenplein, A.J.M. Siza Vieira, 2003-2010   160 m.

Wilhelminakade, Laan op Zuid & environs
T. Koolhaas with various architects
1987-2015

The restructuring of the former docklands at Kop van Zuid saw Rotterdam
city centre extend in the 1980s across
the river Maas to the south bank. The
ambitious programme comprises
some 5000 dwelling units, 380,000
square metres of offices, 50,000
square metres of leisure and cultural
facilities and 3500 square metres of
retail space. It is largely through the
efforts of Riek Bakker, the then director of Rotterdam Town Development,
that the project, masterplanned by
Teun Koolhaas Associates, got off the
ground. An important logistical, but
more especially symbolic, step was
the construction of a new connection between the city centre and South
Rotterdam: the Erasmus Bridge 70.
The programme broadly divides
into two rows of development,
Wilhelminapier and Spoorweghaven,
which meet at right angles. An open
office development has transformed
Wilhelminapier into a 'Manhattan

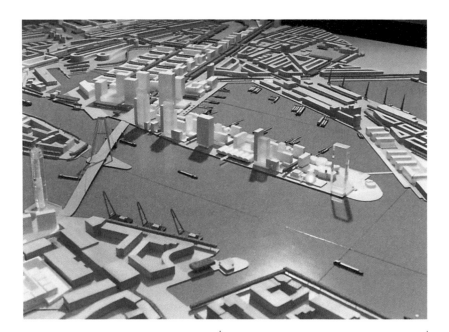

on the Maas'. The largely filled-in Spoorweghaven and the quays along it have been designed as a residential area. Sited at the juncture of the two rows are a clutch of large-scale public facilities, amongst which Wilhelminahof with the law courts, the new Luxor Theatre 🔢 and a new metro station. Dam & Partners' Maastoren is the Netherlands' tallest office building. The area around Entrepothaven is allocated for housing and recreation, the harbour basin itself being given over to yachts. Following construction of the Stadstuinen housing, the strip between Laan op Zuid and Spoorweghaven is being developed with office buildings and Hans Kollhoff's De Compagnie housing complex. Beyond that lies the Parkstad residentlal area.

Buildings

World Port Center, Wilhelminakade 801, Foster and Partners, 1995-2000
Maritime Simulator Centre, Wilhelminakade 701, Foster and Partners, 1993-1994
Housing Boston & Seattle, Otto Reuchlinweg, Van Dongen - Koschuch Architects, 2013-2017
Office Building KPN/Belvédère, Wilhelminakade 123, R. Piano, 1997-2000

Office Building Wilhelminahof, Wilhelminaplein, C.G. Dam, Kraaijvanger. Urbis, 1994-1997
Metro Station Wilhelminahof, Wilhelminaplein, Zwarts & Jansma, 1991-1998
Office Building Maastoren, Wilhelminakade 1, Dam & Partners, 2005-2010
Housing Block Cité, Laan op Zuid/ Veemstraat, Tangram, 2005-2010
Office Building Vancouver, Laan op Zuid, Claus & Kaan, 2006-2009
Housing De Compagnie, Laan op Zuid/ Lodewijk Pincoffsweg, H.F. Kollhoff, 2000-2005
Housing De Evenaar, Halfrond, Cepezed, 1994-1995
Housing Cargadoorskade, Λ.P.J.M. Verheijen, 1995
Housing Stadstuinen, W.G. Witteveenplein & environs, KCAP et al., 1993-2002
Primary school De Pijler, W.G. Witteveenplein 10, KCAP, 1996-1997
Housing Zuiderspoor, Laan op Zuid/Parallelweg, Geurst & Schulze, 2008-2012
Tax Office Building, Laan op Zuid, Van den Oever, Zaaijer & Partners, 2008
Headquarters Sociale Verzekeringsbank Rijnmond, Posthumalaan, Bonnema, 1997-2002

Koninginnenhoofd 1
J. Muller, C.M. Droogleever Fortuyn,
C.B. van der Tak
1901, 1908, 1919
D. de Vos (int. des. 1991-1993)

The headquarters of the Holland-America Line transatlantic shipping company stand at the head of the pier which was once almost exclusively used by the company. The building was erected in phases, the last of which, with its distinctive towers and south elevation decorated with Art Nouveau motifs, was designed by Muller & Zonen and Van der Tak and completed in 1919. On 8 November 1971 the 'Nieuw Amsterdam', the flagship of the HAL, left the quayside for the last time. In 1992, having been empty for years, the office building was restored to its former glory and converted into a hotel cum restaurant (Hotel New York).

Water taxi

Venice and Rotterdam are the only European cities with an extensive water taxi network. Originally established to provide a link between Hotel New York and the right bank of the Maas, the water taxis are firmly entrenched as a rapid and spectacular means of transport. They have their own landing stages and can also make use of Waternet's thirty-plus brightly coloured pontoons designed by Drost + Van Veen.

74   Cruise Terminal

Many of the Holland-America Line sheds were destroyed during the German air raid of May 1940. Of those rebuilt directly after the war only the workshop building and this terminal building for transatlantic passengers by Brinkman, Van den Broek & Bakema remain. The two-storey building has a concrete structure of six shell roofs with an 18 metre span and fully glazed side elevations. Dominating the interior is a monumental stair reaching from the ground-floor luggage department to the passenger zone above.

Wilhelminakade 699
Brinkman, Van den Broek & Bakema
1946-1949

75   Las Palmas

Wilhelminakade 66-68
Van den Broek & Bakema
1950-1953
Benthem Crouwel (ren. 2001-2007)

'Las Palmas' began life as a warehouse cum workshop building, concluding post-war reconstruction for the Holland-America Line complex. It once had a passageway on the ground floor to admit lorries; its concrete frame and the lifts are geared to heavy transport. Open glazed stair halls - a typical feature of Van den Broek & Bakema's architecture - point up the exterior with its cladding of precast concrete elements. Since 2001 Las Palmas has served cultural ends. Since 2007, following alterations made to it by Benthem Crouwel, the complex bears the name Las Palmas and houses a mix of museums, institutes and companies concerned with visual culture. On the roof, which is used for parking, is an office penthouse supported on slim steel columns so that from a distance it appears to float. The volume is horizontal in contrast to the high-rise on Wilhelminapier; the materials and rounded ends allude to shipbuilding.

Emigrants

The Holland-America Line played an important role around 1900 in the emigration of almost a million European migrants headed for America. On Wilhelmina Pier there was a special Emigrants Hotel for East European Jews in particular. After 1945 many Dutch citizens departed from here for economic reasons. The cast-iron memorial, Lost Luggage Depot by Jeff Wall A16, is a reminder of that time.

Rijnhaven

In 2010 Rijnhaven acquired a sustainability pavilion designed by DeltaSync and Public Domain Architects. Moored beside the pavilion is a prototype of the AutArk sustainable floating home. There are also plans for a Floating Wood of twenty tree-buoys designed by Jorge Bakker.

76 Montevideo ☕ 🍴

Montevideo was the Netherlands' tallest residential building when it was completed in 2005. Designed by Francine Houben of Mecanoo, it is intended as a counterpart to the World Port Center on the other side of Hotel New York. Its parts are variously given over to loft, city, sky and water apartments, 192 in all. Not so much apartments as stacked houses, they all boast home automation facilities that include numerous resident services. They share the tower with 6000 square metres of offices, 1900 square metres of shops and restaurants, a health club and a terrace for the residents. All in all, Montevideo is something of a vertical city.

Landverhuizersplein 1-152
F.M.J. Houben (Mecanoo)
1999-2005

77 New Orleans ☕ 🍴

The 160 metre high New Orleans residential tower, with a facade of sand-coloured panels of Chinese granite, was designed by Portuguese architect Alvaro Siza. It has an elegant art deco style crown inspired by the classic New York skyscrapers of the 1930s. The 45 floors contain a total of 234 high-end apartments, varying in size from 65 to 212 square metres; the bigger and more expensive apartments are on the upper floors while the crown houses two luxurious multi-storey penthouses with light wells. Of particular note is the floor height: 2.95 metres. Residents have their own parking space in the underground car park and can make use of such in-house facilities as the four guest suites and the fourth-floor health club. The latter boasts a swimming pool, sauna, fitness room and sun deck on the roof of the low-rise section, which contains the LantarenVenster cinema and jazz club. There is a large multifunctional auditorium on the ground floor and five smaller film theatres on the upper floor.

Van der Hoevenplein
A.J.M. Siza Vieira
2003-2010
ADP Architects (assoc.)

Wilhelminakade 137
OMA
1997-2013

This mixed-use 'vertical city' complex containing offices, apartments, cafés and restaurants was designed way back in 1998, but construction did not commence until 2009 when the city council agreed to become a major tenant of the middle tower. The huge, 149 metre high building with a 100 by 40 metre plinth and a total floor area of 162,000 m², has dominated the skyline of the Wilhelminapier high-rise cluster at Kop van Zuid **72** since its completion. The 40 metre high plinth contains entrance lobbies, a few floors of parking and leisure facilities. On top of the plinth are three inter-connected towers; at around the ninety metre mark the volumes are displaced in different directions. This produces some balconies and cantilevers, but most importantly it articulates the rest of the building mass and manages to create a lively cluster of masses despite the taut and neutral facades. The west tower consists entirely of apartments while the bottom of the east tower is occupied by a hotel.

'Rotterdam is a wind tunnel test that people apparently take part in with great enthusiasm.'

Rem Koolhaas, Vrij Nederland, 14 December 1985

Posthumalaan 1
Bolles + Wilson
1996-2001
Bureau Bouwkunde (assoc.)

Nestling in the heart of Kop van Zuid **72**, the Luxor Theatre abuts the principal local traffic intersection but is also sited along the water. The prevailing colour is red. Its materials and the formal syntax tread a path between robust naval architecture and the intimate and festive theatre ambience. The auditorium is broad and shallow and can accommodate some 1500 theatregoers. Ranged round it is a network of larger and smaller foyers, stairs and refreshment kiosks to encourage the audience to take an informal look round and meet others during intermissions.

Old Luxor

The construction of the new theatre rendered the old Luxor in the city centre redundant. The building at Kruiskade 10 was supposed to be demolished and replaced by a 187 metre high residential tower. The tower plan was shelved and in 2014 the theatre was rehabilitated. The facade was restored to the 1928 situation when the architect A.J. van Wijngaarden built the Luxor Palast with its characteristic light tower. Happily, the ambience of the 1970s refurbishment has been preserved in the large auditorium, including the famous 'love seats' for two.

80　InHolland

Posthumalaan 90
E.L.J.M. van Egeraat
1996-2000

The education building is sited in the row of office buildings along one front with Wilhelminahof. All communal spaces are ranged round an atrium behind a large expanse of glass to profit from the magnificent view across the harbour basin (Rijnhaven). Walkways stitch together the restaurant, study areas and part of the mediatheque. The building consists of two linear zones, a broad glass slab containing the atrium and a narrower relatively closed slab of classrooms. This enclosure is also achieved with glass panels, some of which are blue with a screen-printed pattern. Between 2004 and 2009 the building acquired an additional 15,000 m² in a building that bridges over the metro tunnel and connects with the Cité student housing.

'It's an ugly city, which generates a very healthy humility. Look, when people are overly conscious of being nice, they become unpleasant. It's the same with cities.'

Erick van Egeraat, Elsevier,
8 August 2009

Cité

The university was linked to the Cité student housing via a building rafted over the metro. This building, designed by Tangram Architects, contains close to five hundred flats for local and foreign students and newcomers to the housing market (graduates). Cité consists of two towers of 84 and 75 metres respectively on a podium. The variegated, abstract facade pattern was created by means of variously finished grey-green concrete panels and two window shapes.

Port city

Owing to its location on the Nieuwe Maas river, Rotterdam has always been a port city, but until the nineteenth century its scale remained modest. The docks area lay almost entirely within the historical city triangle between Oudehaven and Leuvehaven, the so-called Waterstad. The crucial impetus for Rotterdam's development as a port city was provided by the construction of the Nieuwe Waterweg canal. Under the guidance of the civil engineer Pieter Caland, a direct, lock-free connection was dug between Rotterdam and the North Sea. The first ship sailed through the Nieuwe Waterweg in 1872 and, with its favourable road, rail and water connections with the hinterland, in particular the German Ruhr, Rotterdam became the Gateway to Europe.

In no time at all big, new docks sprang up on the south bank around the Entrepot Building **82** and the Holland-America Line buildings **73**, **74**, **75**. All the dock basins were excavated; Noordereiland resulted from the digging of Koningshaven, and Katendrecht **85** was formed by the excavation of Rijnhaven and Maashaven. In 1907, work started on Waalhaven, at 310 hectares the largest excavated dock basin in the world. The job was completed in 1931, in the middle of the Depression. The expansion of the port area brought the city prosperity and employment; between 1850 and 1920 the population grew from 90,000 to 515,000.

After the Second World War the port was extended further westwards with Botlek and Europoort. The port now covers an area 40 kilometres in length and includes two large artificial harbours in the sea, Maasvlakte I and II, which are capable of accommodating the largest container ships and tankers. In 1962 Rotterdam displaced New York as the largest port in the world, measured in metric tonnes of cargo throughput. Despite the huge expansion of the port since then, Rotterdam has been overtaken by a few Asian ports: Shanghai, Singapore and Tianjin.

The westward expansion rendered the old docklands in the centre obsolete. Small-scale housing schemes were built on the piers around Leuvehaven and other smaller dock and industrial areas – the DWL District **67**, abattoir, cattle market, Delfshaven Buitendijks – were also re-zoned for residential use. In the 1980s planning commenced for Kop van Zuid **72**, where less than a hundred years earlier the port expansion had begun. The redevelopment has preserved the area's characteristic jetties and historical buildings, and in addition to housing, a new city centre has been created here. Similar dockland and industrial areas on the north bank – Müllerpier **43**, Lloydpier **44**, **45** and Merwe-Vierhavens (M4H) **49** – have also been redeveloped.

Louis Pregerkade, Levie Vorstkade
F.J. van Dongen (de Architekten Cie.)
1991-1997

The tongue of land reaching out between the remaining section of Spoorweghaven and Binnenhaven has been divided into two big apartment buildings separated by a plaza (designed by Atelier Quadrat). The sheer size of the area called for a sturdy, massive architecture and blocks of great sculptural eloquence. The development sites five hefty brickwork blocks between the two harbour basins; the two end blocks are rectangular, the three in-between step up towards Binnenhaven, generating capacious roof gardens for the penthouses. All intermediate areas are closed off with low-rise, except at the plaza.

Shed 24

During the Second World War, Shed 24 on the site of the former Municipal Trade Establishments was used by the German occupying forces as an assembly point for the deportation of 6536 Rotterdam Jews. A remnant of the wall around the Trade Establishments on Stieltjeskade stands in silent testimony. Between the two perimeter blocks on the Land Tongue lies Plein Loods 24, a city square named after the shed. The memorial to the deported Jews is a light element made up of five lighting masts.

☕ 🍴

Handelsplein
Th.J. Stieltjes, A.W. Mees,
J.S.C. van der Wall
1874-1879
Cepezed (ren. 1991-1995)

In a 'vrij entrepot' or free warehouse traders could store goods not directly intended for the Netherlands without having to pay import duties. The free warehouse De Vijf Werelddeelen ('the five continents') is almost 200 metres long and 37 metres wide. The warehouse of over 30,000 m² is divided into five segments each named after a continent. These are separated by heavy fire walls that extend through the facade and the roof. The structure includes cast-iron columns. The complex, separated from its surroundings by a tall blank wall, served as a warehouse until 1990, when it was recast as a shopping centre with office space and housing. A glass-roofed well at its centre floods the building with daylight. Here also are the galleries accessing the housing. The deep units are laid out as lofts and maisonettes, with the wet services freestanding in the 2.85 metre tall apartments.

Pincoffs

The Rotterdam Trade Association or RHV was founded in 1872 by Lodewijk Pincoffs. Between 1874 and 1879 this would grow into the largest trading facility in Europe. Then Pincoffs' empire collapsed; Pincoffs himself fled to America leaving behind a debt running into millions. A statue of Pincoffs was erected in front of the Entrepot Building in 1998 and in 2008 the former customs house at Stieltjesstraat 34 (J.S.C. van der Wall, 1879) became the boutique Suite Hotel Pincoffs. The gateway building is now a house.

83　De Peperklip

Rosestraat, Stootblok, Draaischijf
C.J.M. Weeber (HWST)
1979-1982

One of the most controversial buildings of the last few decades, this
superblock in the shape of an opened-
out paper clip comprises 549 social
housing units. Its rounded end sections contain maisonettes reached
from access galleries; the rest consists
of four levels of porch-accessed flats.
The precast concrete cladding panels
are faced with different-coloured tiles
patterning the facade in such a way
as to make individual units indistin-
guishable. The facade on Rosestraat
bears the inscription 'De Peperklip
Anno 1980' in the tile pictures above
the porches. The Peperklip stands
as a built manifesto for the objec-
tive rationalist architecture and planning formulated by Weeber at the end
of the 1970s. It inveighed against the
cosy 'new frumpishness' (see 59) of
most Dutch housing in that decade,
which Weeber saw as an attempt to
use architecture to disguise the reality of small building budgets in social
housing. Rationalizing the process and
resorting to prefabrication could divert
costs into providing better and more
generously proportioned homes.

'One of the first housing projects built in the harbor
area, this massive, reptilian superblock makes its pre-
sence known and felt, even when viewed from the safe
distance of Google Earth. Built of pre-cast concrete
with colored facades that aggressively refuse to distinguish individual apartments one from the other,
nothing says the end of the 1970s like this rationalist,
harbor-scaled beast marked with the inscription "De
Peperklip Anno 1980."'

Michael Speaks, Rotterdam herzien, 2007

84　The Bridge

Nassaukade 3
JHK Architects, West 8
2000-2004

The head office of Unilever Bestfoods Nederland hovers 26 metres above the existing factory complex on Nassaukade. The rectangular four-storey volume with a base plane of 33 x 130 metres stands on a pair of steel stilts. Brought in by water in sections, the steel structure was assembled on a patch of vacant land and later rolled to its final destination 200 metres further up. The building's architecture took its cue from the diagonal braces required for stability in the facade. A new residential district is projected next door to the factory on the site of the former Oranjeboom brewery at Koningshaven.

Unilever

In 1891, Samuel van den Bergh had relocated his margarine factory from the town of Oss to Nassaukade in Rotterdam, where in 1908 he entered into partnership with a butter trader, also from Oss, Anton Jurgens. In 1930, their Rotterdamse Margarine Unie merged with the British Lever Brothers to form Unilever. Until 1992 the multinational's head office was on Rochussenstraat. Then the company moved into new premises on Weena 4 designed by Jan Hoogstad. The six metre high and fourteen metre wide bronze sculpture 'Corporate Entity' by Wessel Couzijn relocated as well.

2e Katendrechtsehaven
DKV; Maccreanor Lavington
1997-2003; 2000-2002

The Katendrecht peninsula has been successfully transformed from a deprived neighbourhood into a contemporary mix of housing, cafés and restaurants and recreation. Most of the commercial and industrial buildings were demolished around the turn of the millennium. On the land so released 1300 new dwellings were built, doubling the population of the district. The predominantly social housing has been supplemented with apartments, ground-accessed dwellings, self-renovation dwellings and private development plots. Katendrecht once again became an entertainment centre, although the trendy restaurants and theatres around Deliplein have nothing in common with the turbulent sex and drugs scene of the past, with its sailors' cafés, Chinese gambling dens and brothels. A pedestrian bridge connects this nightlife zone with Wilhelminapier. Notable buildings are the housing projects by Maccreanor Lavington and DKV. The main focus of attention of the DKV project are two trapezium-shaped residential towers fully oriented to the water. One has three apartments per floor, the other two. Both towers, which cantilever 12 metres, terminate in two-storey apartments with a roof garden. A low basement and assorted small low-rise blocks of split-level units together enfold a raised plaza above a parking facility. The low-rise portion designed by Maccreanor Lavington consists of 36 back-to-back dwellings with lean-to roofs, hemmed in by four-storey residential blocks containing single-family units and maisonettes.

What's an eager sailor's best bet?
Katendrecht, Katendrecht!
What does he dream of for months on deck?
Of Katendrecht!

Marinus van Henegouwen, song lyrics, 1963

86   SS Rotterdam   ☕ 🍴 🛏 🏛

3e Katendrechtse Hoofd 25
W. Stapel (RDM), C.J. Engelen (HAL)
1952-1959

On September 3rd, 1959, the steam-ship Rotterdam set out on its first transatlantic voyage to New York. Many celebrated artists and architects worked on this flagship of the Holland-America Line built by the Rotterdam Dockyard Company (RDM) 98. The last and largest Dutch ocean liner, it served as a pleasure cruiser between 1971 and 2000. Back in Rotterdam, the vessel now has a permanent moor-ing at Katendrecht 85. It does duty as a congress centre, hotel, restaurant and training centre for two Rotterdam insti-tutes of higher education. The renova-tion, paid for by a housing association, was many times more expensive than estimated.

Cabin boy

When we left Rotterdam that morning,
on the Edam, a sad old tub,
with 'roaches left and right amidships
and rats a'nesting the afore
we had on board a little laddy
that came with us as cabin boy
who sailed the seas the first time
and never heard of sharks before...
And from his Mother on the quayside
he took a shy and bashful leave,
because he didn't dare to kiss her,
that street urchin from Rotterdam...

Anton Beuving, 1940, made famous by
the rendition of Frans van Schaik

Hillekopplein
Mecanoo
1985-1989

Terminating the triangular Afrikaanderwijk area of Rotterdam, this complex consists of a fan-shaped tower looking out over the docks, an undulating block with a gateway and an L-shape completing a perimeter block. This sensitively designed ensemble makes reference to the formal syntax of the moderns; the 16-storey residential tower bears strong similarities to Aalto's Neue Vahr in Bremen. The complex demonstrates that social housing can also lead to high-quality architecture, and so it should.

John Körmeling

The huge green neon numbers 1989 **A13**, the year the Hillekopflat was constructed, were designed by architect/artist John Körmeling. Another permanent work by Körmeling (Pionieer's Hut, 2000) stands on the roof of a customs building in the Rotterdam docklands (Reeweg 16), designed by Benthem Crouwel. The Happy Cloud meeting point in the Rotterdam Central Station concourse **1** is also by Körmeling.

88 Natal

Paul Krugerstraat
F.J. van Dongen (de Architekten Cie.)
1985-1990

A gently winding block with five levels of housing extends across the diagonal of the rectangular site, replacing as it does three small perimeter blocks. It stands on columns to allow visual contact between the public spaces on either side along sight lines running between the shops tucked beneath the building. Orientation of the dwellings is reversed halfway along so that all living rooms look out onto the larger open space. Despite this strategy, which turns the access gallery zone into a row of balconies, Frits van Dongen has achieved a homogeneous facade by wrapping the whole in a concrete grid-like screen.

'Even social housing is entitled to a touch of class.'

Francine Houben, Erick van Egeraat,
Algemeen Dagblad, 6 January 1988

Brielselaan 7/Maashaven Z.z.
J.P. Stok Wzn.
1910
Brinkman & Van der Vlugt
(ext. 1929-1930); AE.G. & J.D. Postma
(ext. 1950-1952)

The silo building designed in 1910 by J.P. Stok at the head of Brielselaan was extended in 1931 by Brinkman & Van der Vlugt with an audacious concrete structure. The brief called for an extension 'so big as to be carried only by the most sturdy foundations imaginable'. These foundations accordingly make use of 'Sprenger' piles with a reinforced point. The steel structure stipulated in the design was replaced by concrete at a late stage, with slip formwork being used for the first time in the Netherlands for the silos and elevator towers. The two silos cantilevering over Brielselaan were added in the early 1950s.

Creative Factory

Since 2003 the silo has been used for house parties and functions. Between 2005 and 2008 it was transformed into the Creative Factory, with office units for young and/or immigrant new entrepreneurs from the worlds of media, fashion, music, design and business services. At the top of the building are two large multifunctional spaces.

90 Purifying Plant

Brielselaan 175
M. Struijs (Public Works)
1990-1993
L. Schouten (artist)

Ever more stringent environmental regulations necessitated the construction at the end of the 1980s of a new plant for purifying flue gas from the city incinerators. The building terminates two urban axes with a flourish. Wrapped around the plant is a tight skin of silver-coloured steel sandwich panels with a dual purpose, to absorb the noise made by the machinery and to ward off wind and weather. The design of the building's curved walls successfully reconciles it with the surroundings, for all its great size. The walls themselves fuse in a dynamic totality that changes appearance with the sun's position in the sky. Having become redundant in 2010, the building will be turned into an amusement park by the well-known entrepreneur from Twente, Hennie van der Most.

Heat Hub

Since 2012 waste heat from the port area has been distributed to households and businesses in the city centre. The so-called Heat Hub, designed as part of the distribution network by WE Architects, absorbs peaks and dips in demand and supply. The two components, a cylindrical buffer tank and a transfer station, are yoked together by a folded roof.

City of architecture

Rotterdam is known as the Netherlands' number one city for architecture. The skyline, the buildings by OMA (21, 35, 78) and MVRDV (25) and Piet Blom's cube dwellings 26 are now major tourist attractions. In 2015, the international Academy of Urbanism proclaimed Rotterdam European City of the Year.

For the general public that city of architecture status may come as something of a surprise. Pre-war Rotterdam was famous for its ugliness and substandard living conditions and even the reconstructed city suffered from a poor image. Among architects, however, Rotterdam has been well thought of since the beginning of the twentieth century. The housing schemes of Michiel Brinkman (51) and J.J.P. Oud (91), the early high-rise experiments of Willem van Tijen (39, 56) and Brinkman & Van der Vlugt's Van Nelle Factory 52 made Rotterdam the cradle of Dutch Modernism.

After the Second World War the city's reconstruction operation was widely admired among town planners. The radical modernization of the city centre was unique in that most cities chose to reconstruct the historical city. The Lijnbaan 12 was a textbook example of a modern shopping centre. A new point of interest in the 1970s was the approach to urban renewal 7, which was widely imitated. There followed the redevelopment of the old port and industrial areas into attractive residential areas like the DWL District 37 and Kop van Zuid 72.

Many well-known architectural practices, such as Van den Broek & Bakema, Maaskant, Quist, Hoogstad, Weeber, OMA, MVRDV and Neutelings Riedijk hail from Rotterdam. The Academies of Art and of Architecture have trained numerous architects. Rotterdam also had the first local architectural activities in the form of the architecture section of the Rotterdam Art Council and ArchiCenter (established in 1992, now UrbanGuides), and it was a pioneer of the annual Architecture Day. The establishment of the Netherlands Architecture Institute (now Het Nieuwe Instituut 31) on Museumpark in 1988 confirmed Rotterdam's status as a city of architecture.

Since the 1970s Rotterdam has also been popular with the creative industry. The many old port and industrial buildings made ideal ateliers for architects, designers, artists and latterly the dance scene as well. The celebrated Van Nelle Factory 52 became the Van Nelle Design Factory. Renamed RDM Campus, the site of the bankrupt Rotterdam Drydock Company 98 has been transformed into a combined hub of education and enterprise.

Every architect starts small with a renovation job or a loft conversion. MVRDV's first built work in Rotterdam was jokingly referred to by the architects as their 'loft conversion', see the picture opposite. This roof extension, dubbed 'Didden Village', is at Beatrijsstraat 71.

1e en 2e Kiefhoekstraat/Lindtstraat
J.J.P. Oud
1925-1930
W. Patijn (rest. 1990-1995)
(Visit museum house,
Hendrik Idoplein 2, via UrbanGuides)

Some 300 dwelling units, two shops, a hot-water service, and a church add up to the Kiefhoek housing estate. Its dwellings were intended for less prosperous workers' families. The plan is based on elongated rows of standardized two-storey units. Having this rational basis respond to its surroundings in different ways gave rise to a varied urban plan. In the south of the estate, the oblique borderline led Oud to design round corners at the acute angle of two open-ended blocks

Church

Oud designed this church serving the Kiefhoek housing free of charge to make sure that nothing of the estate's unity would be lost. Its simple rectangular main space with balconies either side is flanked on one side by ancillary spaces of varying height. Like the houses, the church has white-rendered facades and is horizontally articulated. Only the chimney adds a vertical touch. The church (Eemstein 23) has been renovated, keeping as close as possible to the original design.

containing shops. The horizontally articulated frontage combines a lower band of grey-framed glass with bands of yellow brick. A central white-rendered band divides this from a similarly uninterrupted band of yellow containing fenestration on the upper level. Front gardens are separated from each other by walls of yellow brick and fenced in with blue steel railings. The compact plan (7.5 x 4.1 m.) consists on the ground floor of a living room and entrance porch on the street side and a kitchen facing the garden. A semi-circular stair leads to an upper level of three bedrooms. Lack of funds meant that plans for such facilities as a shower, washbasin, ironing board and service hatch had to be abandoned. Despite this, Oud used the limited means and space available to create a fully-fledged dwelling and boost the 'Existenzminimum' (minimum subsistence level) with an architectural bonus. During a sweeping rehabilitation operation in the early 1990s, all the houses in the district were demolished and meticulously rebuilt, keeping as close as possible to the original design. The Kiefhoek had originally been conceived in concrete, but that was considered too expensive. Experiments with concrete construction were, however, undertaken in the neighbourhoods of De Kossel I and II (Balsemienstraat and Hyacintstraat) by F.G.C. Hulsbosch from 1921-1924 and Stulemeijer I and II (Dortsmondstraat and Walravenstraat) by J.M. van Hardeveld from 1921-1925.

Groenezoom, Lede & environs
M.J. Granpré Molière, P. Verhagen,
A.J.Th. Kok
1913-1942
(Visit museum house, Lede 40, via
www.museumvreewijk.nl)

Vreewijk, Rotterdam's first garden village, was the brainchild of the banker K.P. van der Mandele. He bought a patch of land in South Rotterdam and commissioned Berlage to draw up an urban plan for it. Unlike Heijplaat 98, Vreewijk had no connection with a particular company. Many office clerks, council officials and teachers lived here alongside manual labourers. Berlage's design, its angled street pattern retaining the original watercourses on site, was fleshed out from 1916 on by Granpré Molière, Verhagen & Kok and De Roos & Overeijnder. As it was wartime and material was scarce, the building process took a long time to get going. A total of 5700 houses were built between 1917 and 1942. Vreewijk has always been regarded as the traditional counterpart of modernist districts such as Kiefhoek 91. Vreewijk's buildings are indeed traditional in that they are built of brick in a site layout that makes a clear distinction between street and courtyard, but they also admit to a standardization of dwelling types and to a construction process efficiently organized along modernist lines. Most of the houses are assembled in open blocks in a north-south alignment. Much thought has been given to street profiles (the width of streets as against that of the pavement), building height and the position of trees, lampposts and garden hedges and walls. Greenery prevails in this garden village. The district's centre is the Brink or village green with its 'People's House'. There are shops, schools and churches but there were no cafés. Granpré Molière himself regarded the architecture as rather shabby, even if 'bedecked with nature's mantle'. Since the 1980s many houses have been renovated with little regard for the existing architecture; in 2014 Vreewijk became a national monument.

'Vreewijk Garden Village. Example of a well-designed and well-kept development. While on the right bank of the Maas many a fine old country house has been demolished over the years, here in the open landscape a new garden city is growing, with all the attractions of low-density development. If it proves possible to extend the character of this planning, the South will indeed have a delightful appearance.'

Ir. Alph. Siebers, Groeiend Rotterdam, 1929

93 Essalam Mosque

Vredesplein 7
Molenaar & Van Winden
2002-2011

Plans to build the Essalam Mosque with its two 50 metre tall minarets caused no end of fuss among locals and politicians. Traditional in layout, this mosque was designed for the Moroccan community by the thoroughly Dutch architects Molenaar & Van Winden. Its concrete structure has a cladding of stone panels. The ground floor contains the non-religious amenities including a shop and activity rooms. The men's prayer rooms are on the first floor. The third floor, which is where the women pray, also has the library, the imam's room and offices and classrooms. A central well below the dome ties all these spaces together.

Exotic places of worship

Rotterdam has always had many international churches, for refugees and sailors:

Norwegian Seamen's Church, Westzeedijk 300, M. Poulsson & A. Arneberg, 1914
St. Mary's Church, Pieter de Hoochweg 133, J. Verheul Dzn., 1913-1915
l'Eglise Wallonne, Schiedamse Vest 190, J. Verheul Dzn., J. van Wijngaarden, 1923-1925
Scots International Church, Schiedamse Vest 121, M.C.A. Meischke, 1951-1953
Synagogue, A.B.N. Davidsplein 2-4, J. van Duin, St. van Duin & Jac.S. Baars, 1951-1954
Greek Orthodox Church, Westzeedijk 333, Th.J. Taen, Ch.Th. Nix, 1947-1957
Danish Seamen's Church, Coolhaven 1-7, H. Jensen, N.L. Prak, 1968-1970
Mevlana Mosque, Mevlanaplein 1, H.W.D. Toorman (Heuvelhorst Architects), 1995-2001
Russian Orthodox Church, Schiedamsesingel 220, L. Waardenburg, 1994-2004

Van Zandvlietplein 1
Brinkman & Van der Vlugt
1934-1936
Zwarts & Jansma, ABT (ren. 1993-1994)

'De Kuip' ('The Tub') has a lower and an upper level of terraces whose continuous curves follow the pitch so as to keep the distance between spectator and game to a minimum. Roofing and upper level are suspended from a cantilevered steel lattice structure. Some 65,000 spectators are able to vacate the stadium in six minutes flat via 22 double steel stairs on its outer face. During a restoration in 1994, the 60-year-old stadium was provided with a new structurally independent roof placed over rather than on the existing component.

Hendrik Chabot

The statue The Footballer by the expressionist Rotterdam artist Hendrik Chabot was greeted with general scepticism in 1937. The art critics would have preferred a more athletic figure and the fans gave it rather unflattering nicknames like Manus Gorilla and Jan with the hands. Chabot had deliberately chosen to make a scrawny, rugged figure because football was a working man's sport. Nowadays the reinforced concrete statue is cherished by football fans and art experts alike.

95 Plussenburgh

Grote Hagen 566-772
Arons & Gelauff
2004-2006

Here, two oblong portions configured as a vertical cross contain 104
apartments for over 55s. The horizontal part is held aloft on V-shaped pairs
of columns standing in an ornamental pool. Below this part, in the water,
is the central recreation room. Various
other communal amenities occupy the
ground floor. There is a parking facility for 51 cars below the site, accessed
down a spiral ramp. But the most striking features are the undulating balconies whose horizontal floor slabs

and vertical partitions wind their way
over the facade at distances that vary
between 0.8 and 2.4 metres. This
undulating effect is strengthened by
the balcony railings which sway to and
fro to the rhythm of the floor slabs.

Zonnetrap

Nearby in Lombardijen, at Molenvliet
206-640, stands an older senior housing
complex by the architects Enrico and
Luzia Hartsuyker. The 1980 building is
based on the Biopolis study, a critique
of CIAM urban design in the form of
mega structures containing a range
of integrated functions. The terraced
arrangement of the 179 dwellings and the
combination with orthogonal blocks for
offices, studios and shared facilities deliv-
ers a fascinating spatial configuration in
the indoor areas.

96 The Black Pearl

Pompstraat 44
Rolf.fr, Zecc Architects
2007-2010

Self-renovation houses, marketed individually and collectively, seem to be particularly in vogue with newcomers to the housing market and fulfil the bureaucratic aim of luring young, affluent households to unpopular problem neighbourhoods. Industrial designer Rolf Bruggink transformed an old building in Charlois into a dizzying system of voids, floors and stairs where only the chipped outer brick walls appear to have been retained. The side elevation was clad with artificial grass and the front facade was painted black after which two stainless steel windows were inserted.

Self-renovation houses

'Rotterdam is giving houses away for free!' It was with this provocative slogan that the phenomenon of 'self-renovation houses' was introduced in the Spangen district in late 2004. It is an unusual form of urban regeneration in which dilapidated houses in old districts are offered for sale for a very low price, on condition that the buyer renovate the dwelling. Well-known collective renovation projects include the Wallisblok on Wallisweg in Spangen and Eén blok stad on Zwaerdecroonstraat in Middelland.

97 Pendrecht

Slinge/Zuiderparkweg/Groene Kruisweg
C.I.A. Stam-Beese
1949-1953
J.B. Bakema (assoc.)

Pendrecht, one of the districts built on Rotterdam's southern rim during the post-war reconstruction, was originally intended to house those working in the nearby docks. The fascinating thing about Pendrecht is the attempt it makes to organize its 6300 dwellings using an ascending series of spatial units: dwelling, cluster, neighbourhood, district, town. The district configures four neighbourhoods around a traffic-free square. Instead of the usual system of perimeter blocks or series of freestanding apartment buildings, the fundamental unit chosen for these neighbourhoods was the so-called *wooneenheid* (cluster), which can be considered a spatial and social link between home and neighbourhood. Each cluster consists of a mix of buildings catering to differing categories of resident. This social diversity is reflected in their spatial layout of freestanding blocks of differing height together surrounding a communal green space. The schools are accommodated in the district's centre and in a green zone linking this centre with Zuiderpark 65 to the north. Shops are partly located centrally and partly decentralized throughout the scheme.

The fishbowls

Pendrecht did not escape the fate that befell most post-war districts. Its one-sided housing stock was a magnet for the socially vulnerable, precipitating the model neighbourhood into a downward spiral. Large parts of Pendrecht have been torn down in recent years, with low-cost social housing being replaced by more expensive owner-occupied properties. However, the 'fishbowl units' designed by Harry Nefkens have been renovated.

Rondoplein & environs
H.A.J. Baanders
1914-1918
S. de Clercq
(ext. 1924-1928, 1930, 1938)

In 1902 the Rotterdam Dockyard Company (RDM) began its career with a new wharf at Heijplaat. Ship repairs were the main bill of fare, although spectacular new ships like the Nieuw Amsterdam (1937) and the SS Rotterdam 86 (1959) were built here. Seven thousand people were employed here in the 1970s. The first workers' district in Rotterdam built in accordance with the garden city concept owes its existence to De Gelder, director of the RDM. Wedged between the Waalhaven and Heysehaven basins, Heijplaat was set up to house skilled dock workers near the shipyard. The first phase of building produced 400 houses, two churches, a community centre with shops, two schools, a library, a wash- and bathhouse and an after-work centre including a café and a theatre. After only a few years the district was expanded to the south. A further extension followed in the 1950s. Local protests against a proposal to demolish Heijplaat led to wholesale renovation in the 1980s.

RDM Campus

The RDM wharf went bankrupt in 1983 and again in 2004. Today the RDM area with its facilities for education and conferences, offices and artists' studios, is dedicated to encouraging creative activity. RDM now stands for Research Design & Manufacturing. The Academy of Architecture occupies the old main building while the Innovation Dock (the former Machine Hall) is home to a concentration of professional and vocational courses and businesses. The huge former Torpedo Shed is used for exhibitions and cultural events.

99 WiMBY!

Various locations
Various architects
2000-2007

Since 1947, when Hoogvliet was still a village, this satellite town southwest of Rotterdam has expanded with some 15,000 housing units, mainly for workers at the nearby docks and refineries. Hoogvliet now consists of a centre with eight districts, each roughly the size of Pendrecht 97, ranged round it concentrically. A low embankment at the old village church is all that remains of its past. A modern open layout with many walk-up blocks now prevails. There is so much public green space that at the end of the 1960s Hoogvliet with its 40 square metres per inhabitant was the greenest settlement in the Netherlands. A Lijnbaanesque 12 shopping centre was built in the central area in the mid '60s. A metro line laid out in 1974 links Hoogvliet with

Rotterdam. By the turn of the millennium Hoogvliet, more than any other product of post-war reconstruction with a one-sided housing stock, had acquired a negative image because of racial tension and crime. The necessary restructuring requires demolishing 5000 cheap, poor quality housing units and then building almost as many new units. The existing structures (district, traffic, green space) have largely been retained in the new urban layout. An acronym for Welcome into My Backyard, WiMBY! is an independent organization entrusted with supervising the restructuring of Hoogvliet. WiMBY! has developed and put in place a rich mix of experimental buildings, small projects and joint ventures relating to architecture, urban design, visual art and sociocultural projects.

Visible results of renewal in Hoogvliet

Housing Block De Condor, Digna Johannaweg 141-237, Zeinstra Van der Pol, 2005-2007
Housing Alverstraat, VMX Architects, 2004-2007
Pavilion De Villa/Heerlijkheid Hoogvliet, Herikweg 5, FAT Architecture, 2001-2008
Campus Hoogvliet, Lengweg, Wiel Arets Architects, 2007-2014
Co-housing Hof van Heden, Doradehof, Opmaat, 2006-2010
Co-housing Veld van Klanken, Marlijnstraat, 24H architecture, 2006-2010
Co-housing Nabuurschap, Tarbotstraat, Van Bergen Kolpa, 2006-2010
Accent Praktijkschool, Max Havelaarweg 53, VMX Architects, 2010-2011

100 Nesselande

Laan van Avant-Garde & environs
Dept. of Urban Design and Housing,
with various architects
2001-2012

Rotterdam's latest residential district is sited on land annexed from the municipality of Nieuwerkerk aan den IJssel, with a metro line as its only link to the city. Built as part of the Vinex urban development programme, it consists mainly of middle and higher income housing. Its housing reflects the current trend of thought in the Netherlands and in that respect is typical Vinex. At its centre is a two kilometre long green zone of watercourses and ecological shores. Here too are the electricity masts and the elevated metro line which ends at a terminal. Local facilities - shopping centre, community centre, library, health centre - are concentrated here near the metro station in a spatial plan by Spanish urban designer Joan Busquets. The centre is located close to the beach of Zevenhuizerplas and the architecture here aspires to a Mediterranean ambience. The polder setting inspired a 'water district' of 500 plots free from aesthetic controls; the houses sit on islands and have a landing stage for a small boat.

Buildings in Nesselande

Community School/Seniors Housing, Robert van 't Hoffstraat, Cita Architects, 2000-2005
Metro Station Nesselande, Laan van Dada, H. Moor, 2000-2006
Water Dwellings Nesselande, Marinus van Elswijkkade, J. Vos, 2003-2006
Housing Herman Bielingplein, Claus & Kaan, 2000-2007
Housing Duinenbuurt, Siciliëboulevard/Kretalaan, Groosman/Burobeb/Vasco da Silva, 2002-2008
Housing block Barcelona, Siciliëboulevard, J. Busquets, 2005-2007
Cultural Centre De Kristal, Corsicalaan/Mallorcastraat, Meyer & Van Schooten, 2005-2008
Housing block Miami, Siciliëboulevard, Meyer & Van Schooten, 2004-2010
Housing block Kopenhagen, Siciliëboulevard, 3xNielsen, 2005-?

Index of buildings